Structured Exercises in

Management

Volume
4

Structured Exercises in

Management

A Handbook for
Trainers, Educators, Group Leaders

Volume

4

Edited by
Nancy Loving Tubesing, EdD
Donald A Tubesing, MDiv, PhD

Library of Congress Cataloging in Publication Data

Structured exercises in stress management : A handbook for trainers, educators, and
  group leaders / Nancy Loving Tubesing and Donald A. Tubesing, eds.
  192p. 23cm.
    Summary: A collection of thirty-six exercises for stress management to be used
  by trainers and facilitators in group settings.
    ISBN 1-57025-017-0 (v.4 : pbk) : $29.95
    1. Stress (psychology)—Prevention, problems, exercises, etc. 2. Stress—
  Psychological, prevention & control, problems. I. Title. II. Tubesing, Nancy
  Loving III. Tubesing, Donald A.
  BF575.S75S74   1986, 1990 1994
  158'.92—dc19   83-61073

Printed in the United States of America

10 9 8 7 6 5 4 3 2 1

Published by:

WHOLE PERSON ASSOCIATES
210 West Michigan
Duluth MN 55802
(800) 247-6789

PREFACE

Over a decade ago we launched an experiment in health education—the Whole Person series of **Structured Exercises in Stress Management** *and* **Structured Exercises in Wellness Promotion**. *We believed that it was time to move beyond peptalks and handouts to an experiential approach that actively involves the participant—as a whole person—in the learning process.*

What began as an experiment has become a catalyst for dramatic changes in health promotion and education! **Structured Exercises** *volumes have found their way into the libraries of trainers, consultants, group workers, and health professionals around the world. We're proud that these volumes have become classics—the resource of choice for planning stress management and wellness promotion programs.*

Our purpose in publishing this series was to foster inter-professional networking and to provide a framework though which we can all share our most effective ideas with each other. As you will soon discover, we scoured the country looking for the most innovative, effective teaching designs used by the most creative consultants and trainers in business, health care and social services, then included some of their most imaginative ideas in this volume.

Many of the exercises we designed ourselves and refined in hundreds of workshops we've conducted over the past twenty years. Some are new combinations of time-tested group process activities. Others were submitted by people like you who continually strive to add the creative touch to their teaching.

The layout of **Structured Exercises** *is designed for easy photocopying of worksheets, handouts and preparation notes. Please take advantage of our generous policy for reproduction—but also please be fair to the creative individuals who have so generously shared their ideas with you.*

☞ *You may duplicate worksheets and handouts for use in training or educational events—as long as you use the proper citation as indicated on the copyright page. Please also give written credit to the original contributor. Whenever we've been able to track down the source of an idea, we've noted it. Please do the same when you share these ideas with others.*

☞ *However, all materials in this volume are still protected by copyright. Prior written permission from Whole Person Press is required if you plan large scale reproduction or distribution of any portion of this book. If you wish to include any material or adaptation in another publication, you must have permission in writing before proceeding. Please send us your request and proposal at least thirty days in advance.*

Structured Exercises *are now available in two convenient formats. This small-format softcover version is produced with a new book binding process that stays open on your desk or podium for easy reference, and lies flat on the photocopier for quick duplication of worksheets.*

Many trainers enjoy the wide margins and larger type of the full-size looseleaf format, which provides plenty of space for you to add your own workshop designs, examples, chalktalk notes, and process reminders for your presentations. The looseleaf version also includes a complete package of camera-ready worksheet masters for easy reproduction of professional-looking handouts.

☞ *See page 152 in the Resources section for complete descriptions and ordering information for worksheet masters and companion volumes of the* **Stress** *and* **Wellness** *series in softcover and loose-leaf formats.*

We are grateful to the many creative trainers who have so generously shared their "best" with you in this volume (see page 145) as well as others in the series. We hope that the ideas here stimulate your own creative juices.

So, go ahead. Strive to bring your teaching alive in new ways. Expand your stress management approach. Continue to touch and motivate people with learning experiences that engage and challenge them as whole persons.

Then let us know what works well for you. We'd love to consider your new ideas for inclusion in a future volume so that we can carry on the tradition of providing this international exchange of innovative teaching designs.

Duluth MN   *Nancy Loving Tubesing*
January 1994   *Donald A Tubesing*

INTRODUCTION

Stress is a fact of life—and from the board room to the emergency room to the living room people are searching for ways to manage stress more positively.

Structured Exercises in Stress Management, Volume 4 offers you 36 designs you can use for helping people move beyond information to implementation. Each exercise is structured to creatively involve people in the learning process, whatever the setting and time constraints, whatever the sophistication of the audience. To aid you in the selection of appropriate exercises, they are grouped into six broad categories:

> *Icebreakers:* These short (10–20 minutes) and lively exercises are designed to introduce people to each other and to the subject of stress management. Try combining an icebreaker with an exercise from the assessment or management section for an instant evening program.

> *Stress Assessments:* These exercises explore the symptoms, sources and dynamics of stress. All the processes help people examine the impact of stress in their lives. You'll find a mixture of shorter assessments (30–60 minutes) and major theme developers (60–90 minutes). Any exercise can easily be contracted or expanded to fit your purpose.

> *Management Strategies:* Each of these processes explores the issue of overall strategies for dealing with the stress of life. Participants evaluate their strengths and weaknesses and identify skills for future development.

> *Skill Developers:* Each volume in this handbook series will focus on a few coping skills in more depth. The four exercises in this section highlight relaxation, surrender, laughter and interpersonal contact skills.

> *Action Planning/Closure:* These exercises help participants draw together their insights and determine the actions they wish to take on their own behalf. Some also suggest rituals that bring closure to the group process.

> *Energizers:* The energizers are designed to perk up the group whenever fatigue sets in. Sprinkle them throughout your program to illustrate skills or concepts. Try one for a change of pace—everyone's juices (including yours!) will be flowing again in 5–10 minutes.

The format is designed for easy use. You'll find that each exercise is described completely, including: goals, group size, time frame, materials needed, step-by-step process instructions, and variations.

    ☞ *Special instructions for the trainer and scripts to be read to the group are typed in italics.*

    ✔ Questions to ask the group are preceded by a check.

    ➤ Directions for group activities are indicated by an arrow.

    ● Mini-lecture notes are preceded by a bullet.

Although the processes are primarily described for large group (25 to 100 people) workshop settings, most of the exercises work just as well with small groups, and many are appropriate for individual therapy or personal reflection.

If you are teaching in the workshop or large group setting, we believe that the use of small discussion groups is the most potent learning structure available to you. We've found that groups of four persons each provide ample air time and a good variety of interaction. If possible, let groups meet together two or three different times during the learning experience before forming new groups.

These personal sharing groups allow people to make positive contact with each other and encourage them to personalize their experience in depth. On evaluations, some people will say "Drop this," others will say, "Give us more small group time," but most will report that the time you give them to share with each other becomes the heart of the workshop.

If you are working with an intact group of 12 people or less, you may want to keep the whole group together for process and discussion time rather than divide into the suggested four or six person groups.

Each trainer has personal strengths, biases, pet concepts and processes. We expect and encourage you to expand and modify what you find here to accommodate your style. Adjust the exercises as you see fit. Bring these designs to life for your participants by inserting your own content and examples into your teaching. Experiment!

And when you come up with something new, let us know . . .

CONTENTS

ICEBREAKERS

STRESS ASSESSMENTS

MANAGEMENT STRATEGIES

SKILL BUILDERS

PLANNING & CLOSURE

GROUP ENERGIZERS

RESOURCES

Icebreakers

109 INTRODUCTIONS 8

In these two get-acquainted exercises participants compare their stress management styles to different dance steps (**Coping Choreography**) and find a weather forecast to fit their mood (**Barometer**).

GOALS

To get acquainted.

To provoke discussion on topics related to stress management.

GROUP SIZE

Unlimited. With large groups (more than 20 people), divide into smaller (6–12 people) groups for introductions.

TIME FRAME

10–20 minutes. Allow more time for larger groups.

PROCESS

Introduction A: COPING CHOREOGRAPHY

1) The trainer invites participants to focus on a particular event, situation or life condition that has been causing them stress recently (eg, a hassle at work, difficulty in a relationship, financial pressures, etc).

   ☞ *Give people a minute to get focused, then ask if anyone needs more time. If so, suggest they recall the little challenges they faced today just to get here.*

2) As soon as everyone has a specific stressor in mind, the trainer describes the introduction process:

   ➤ Imagine what type of dance or dance step typifies your stress management style for dealing with that stress.

   ☞ *Give a few examples (eg, "Has it been more like a hula or a jitterbug? A tap dance or a waltz?"). If the group seems confused or resistant, try brainstorming a list of dance steps (eg, two-step, polka, soft shoe, disco, twist, break dance, cha-cha, can-can, ballet, minuet, jig, reel, swing, square dance, etc).*

> In a moment we will introduce ourselves. When it's your turn, give your name, then disclose the dance you selected and say something about how your coping style resembles that step.

   ☞ *The trainer should begin the process by introducing yourself, identifying your dance step, and sharing how it fits your stress management style.*

3) After all have shared, the trainer makes a few comments before moving on to a more intensive examination of stress and/or coping.

● Like a dance, our lives are composed of patterns repeated over and over. Our typical patterns and habitual styles of managing stress may feel comfortable, even when they are not effective.

● The purpose of a stress management course like this one is to learn some new patterns, to add variety and flexibility, to allow us to "dance" to more kinds of music.

Introduction B: BAROMETER

1) The trainer asks participants to reflect on the climate of their life recently and to choose a weather condition that corresponds to their current lifestyle (eg, *fair and mild, blizzard warning, heat wave, scattered showers, high winds*).

2) Participants introduce themselves, identify their weather condition and briefly describe why it fits their life right now.

   ☞ *Give a few good examples to stimulate creativity (eg, "I feel like I am under a tornado warning—chaotic, apprehensive, just waiting for disaster to strike" or "I feel partly cloudy—life is pretty upbeat for me right now, but I have a few worries that bother me occasionally").*

   You may want to introduce yourself first to set the pace and disclosure level.

110 FAMILY YARNS

In this nostalgic get-acquainted exercise, participants compare notes on novel and imaginative responses to stress.

GOALS

To get acquainted.

To consider the sources of family stress and family members' strengths in dealing with it.

GROUP SIZE

Unlimited. With large groups (more than 20 people), divide into smaller (6–12 people) groups for introductions.

TIME

10–20 minutes. Allow more time for larger groups.

MATERIALS

Blank 4"x6" note cards, crayons or felt-tip markers, a 2–3 foot length of yarn for each participant, paper punch.

PROCESS

1) The trainer gives each participant a 4"x6" notecard and a piece of yarn, and distributes crayons, markers and a paper punch at strategic locations around the group.

2) Participants are instructed to make a name tag for themselves:

   ➤ First, draw a line down the middle of your card. Think for a minute about your family and your experiences growing up in that environment. On the left side of the card write down three things that caused you or your family stress at some point (eg, commuting, financial worries, nosy neighbors, a new baby, fighting, alcohol use, etc).

   ☞ *Give people time here to focus clearly on three family stressors.*

   ➤ Now I'd like you to expand your focus and let your mind wander to your wider family of all generations. Bring to mind one of your relatives (adult or child) who has attempted to cope with stress in an imaginative or unusual way (eg, blaming it on the dog, hiding under the bed, writing poetry, etc).

➤ Write that person's name on the right side of your card and jot down a few words about their unusual coping style.

    ☞ *If people seem to be having trouble, reassure them that the coping technique doesn't have to be outrageous. Suggest that they just imagine one person (eg, mother, spouse, cousin) and describe their typical style.*

➤ Finally, turn your card over and use the crayons and markers to make a name tag. Print your first name only in large letters and decorate it any way that you like. Then punch holes in the card, string the yarn through and tie it. Voila! Put on your name tag necklace.

3) The trainer reassembles the group and invites participants to introduce themselves by telling their "family yarns." One by one, people reveal family stressors and tell stories about family members' unusual styles of coping.

VARIATION

■ In a larger group participants can join in trios for the first part of *Step 3*, introducing themselves and comparing notes on family stressors. After five minutes, the trainer directs the trios to join with two other trios to make groups of nine. (Extra trios should make sextets.) In this larger group, people introduce themselves again, this time telling the story of their relatives' offbeat approaches to managing stress.

111 QUIPS AND QUOTES

Participants introduce themselves using memorable quotations, then join forces in trios to create tongue-in-cheek definitions of stress.

GOALS

To promote interaction among participants.

To demonstrate the benefits of a light-hearted approach to a serious subject.

GROUP SIZE

Unlimited, as long as there is space for trios to meet comfortably.

TIME FRAME

20–30 minutes

MATERIALS

Quips and Quotes handouts for everyone. Newsprint sheets and markers for each trio.

PROCESS

1) The trainer announces that participants will spend the next half hour getting acquainted and approaching the subject of stress from an unusual angle.

   She distributes **Quips and Quotes** handouts to everyone and gives instructions for choosing a quotation.

   ➤ Read through this list of quotations, proverbs and maxims.

   ➤ As you read, mark in the margin every quote that sparks your interest in any way (eg, tickles your funny bone, sounds like good advice for your spouse, reminds you of the last six weeks, etc). Don't worry about why the saying strikes you, just mark it.

2) After 3–5 minutes the trainer asks participants to choose one quote to use as an introduction of themselves in the group.

   ☞ *If the group is larger than 15, divide into groups of 8–12 people for this phase of the introductions.*

➤ Pick one saying that stands out for you, that has special meaning. It could:

    Represent the current stress in your life;
    Contain some good advice for you;
    Typify your approach to stress management;
    Provide comfort or amusement;
    Or any other reason you might have.

➤ Everyone will have about one minute to tell your name, share your quote and tell us something about its meaning for you.

3) After everyone has been introduced the trainer solicits definitions and examples of stress from the group by asking:

✔ When you use the word stress, what do you mean?

☞ *Encourage people to be specific about stressors and generate as broad a range of definitions as you can in 1–2 minutes.*

4) The trainer notes that most of these definitions and examples are serious, yet the group's choices of quotes were mostly humorous. She comments that humor can take the punch out of stress, and offers this light-hearted definition of stress:

● Stress is the confusion created when one's mind overrides the body's desire to choke the living daylights out of some jerk who desperately needs it.

5) The trainer announces that during the next 10 minutes participants will join in small groups to compose their own clever definitions of stress.

➤ Find two other people who share at least one letter in common with your first or last name. As soon as you have a trio, find space where you can work comfortably together, then sit down. Send a representative from your group to get some newsprint and markers.

☞ *Allow time for people to get settled before moving to the next instruction. If there are one or two extra folks, have them join trios to make quartets.*

➤ Spend about five minutes together brainstorming possible ideas and examples of stressful situations seen in a humorous light. Use the paradigm *Stress is* . . . and record all your ideas on the newsprint.

☞ *Give a few examples here to prime the pump (eg, "Stress is a 3-and-2 count with two outs in the bottom of the ninth." "Stress is having eyes bigger than your stomach." "Stress is a Valium deficiency." "Stress is your boss asking, 'Got a minute?'").*

➤ I'll call time in five minutes and give further instructions.

6) After about five minutes the trainer interrupts the process and describes the next step.

➤ Look over your group's list of definitions and decide for yourself which two you like best.

➤ Privately, each person should spend the next three minutes quietly revising, rewriting, editing, polishing your two favorites. Use the back of your **Quips and Quotes** handout to record your process.

➤ I'll call time in a few minutes and give further instructions. Please respect the creative process of your neighbors by maintaining a strict silence during this time.

7) After a few minutes the trainer breaks the silence and instructs the trios to reconvene, share their definitions, and choose one or two samples of their collected wisdom to read to the entire group. (2 minutes)

8) The trainer gathers all participants and asks each trio to share their best definitions of stress with the whole group. After all groups have had a turn in the spotlight, participants are encouraged to give each other a round of applause for their creativity.

VARIATIONS

■ As part of *Step 6* people could write each of their definitions on a notecard. At the end of the experience, the trainer collects all the cards and posts them on the wall for others to study at their leisure. Definitions could also be duplicated and distributed to all participants at a later date.

■ Trios in *Step 8* could make a poster of their favorite definition, decorating it with appropriate drawings, symbols, etc. After sharing with the big group, trios hang the posters around the room to remind everyone that stress is too important to take seriously!

QUIPS AND QUOTES

A crisis is a shortcut to the future—not the end of the world.

Don't sweat the small stuff. It's all small stuff.

Work expands so as to fill the time available for its completion.
(Parkinson's Law)

I've had a lot of trouble in my life, most of which never happened.
(Mark Twain)

Procrastination is the art of keeping up with yesterday.

The great end of life is not knowledge but action.   (TH Huxley)

I have found the best way to give advice to your children is to find out what they want and then advise them to do it.   (Harry Truman)

Speak when you're angry—and you'll make the best speech you'll ever regret.

The time to relax is when you don't have time for it.

Children are unpredictable. You never know what inconsistency they're going to catch you in next.

To kill time, a committee is the perfect weapon.

Be pleasant until ten o'clock in the morning and the rest of the day will take care of itself.

It is a luxury to be understood.   (Ralph Waldo Emerson)

People who say they sleep like a baby usually don't have one.

People ask you for criticism but they only want praise.   (Somerset Maugham)

Habit is the easiest way to be wrong again.

Insanity is hereditary—you get it from your kids.

To err is human, but when the eraser wears out ahead of the pencil, you're overdoing it.

The secret of dealing successfully with a child is not to be its parent.

If you don't get what you want, want what you get.

To have a stress-free day, take a night job.

We hope vaguely but dread precisely.

Not to decide is to decide.

Why not put off worrying about today until tomorrow? By then it will be yesterday.

H.S.I.O.W.—Holy cow! It's only Wednesday!   (George Carlin)

When you think you're about to go to pieces, pour glue all over yourself.

When stress takes its toll, ask for a receipt.

The time you enjoy wasting is not wasted time.

An optimist expects dreams to come true; a pessimist expects nightmares to.

Life is what happens to us while we're making other plans.

Remember, no one can make you feel inferior without your consent.
                    (Eleanor Roosevelt)

It's better to have loved and lost than to do ten loads of laundry a week.

Life can only be understood backwards; but it must be lived forwards.
                    (Soren Kierkegaard)

The great secret of a successful marriage is to treat all the disasters as incidents and none of the incidents as disasters.

The best thing about the future is that it comes only one day at a time.
                    (Abe Lincoln)

Man is born into trouble as the sparks fly upward.   (Job 5:7)

Dear God, I pray for patience. And I want it **right now!**

It isn't that I can't see the solution. I can't see the problem!

Do not take life too seriously. You'll never get out of it alive.

Hope for the best, prepare for the worst and take what comes.

The sooner you fall behind the more time you have to catch up.

If we learn from our mistakes, I ought to be a genius.

Try to relax and enjoy the crisis.

If you can't go around it, over it, or through it, you had better negotiate with it.

Please don't tell me to relax—it's only my tension that's holding me together.

Even God cannot change the past.

The longest journey begins with a single step.

112 COUNT FIVE

In this zany introduction, participants share stress perceptions and exchange coping tips as they weave around the circle.

GOALS

To promote interaction and help participants get acquainted.

To focus attention on personal stressors and coping techniques in a non-threatening manner.

GROUP SIZE

Works best with 20 or more participants.

TIME FRAME

10–15 minutes

MATERIALS

Enough unobstructed space so that participants can easily make one large circle.

PROCESS

☞ *This exercise can be chaotic and fun, especially with a large group. Be sure you understand the process and practice it with a friendly group before you spring it on a group of strangers.*

1) The trainer begins by inviting participants to stand and join him in making one large circle, facing inward.

2) As soon as the circle is formed, the trainer starts the **Count Five** exercise, explaining the process as he demonstrates it.

☞ *Step inside the circle and walk through each part of the process while you explain it.*

➤ Walk around the circle to your right (counterclockwise) counting each person out loud: 1, 2, 3, 4, 5.

➤ At the fifth person, stop, shake hands, introduce yourself and quickly tell that person one stress you've experienced in the last week.

➤ Send that person off ***clockwise*** while you continue ***counter-clockwise*** around the circle.

☞ *As you and your "fifth" demonstrate this step check to make sure everyone understands the process. Continue with the rest of the instructions as you act them out.*

➤ Each person **Counts Five** (in opposite directions), then stops for handshakes, introductions and stressor exchange with the fifth person.

➤ Send that person off in the opposite direction to **Count Five** while you continue to move and **Count Five**. Don't forget to share stressors—including the stress of doing this !

☞ *There should be 4 people moving around the circle at this point, 8 people after the next introductions, 16 after the next, etc. At some point everyone around the circle will have been designated as a "fifth" and sent on the way to Count Five.*

3) Just before the last participants leave the circle to start counting five, the trainer interrupts to give further instructions.

➤ You may have noticed there's no one left in the circle. No problem! Just keep moving around the group counting five and introducing yourself until I interrupt you again. See if you can think of some new stresses from the past week to talk about.

4) After 3–5 more minutes of milling around the trainer directs people to gather a group of five people by counting five (including themselves).

☞ *In a large group announce that "leftovers" should move to the center of the room to find other stragglers. If fewer than four are without a group, suggest they split up and each join a different group.*

5) The trainer instructs participants in the small groups to introduce themselves again—at a more leisurely pace. This time they are asked to share two or three of their typical ways of handling stress.

6) After 5–8 minutes, the trainer reconvenes the entire group and before moving on to the next part of the agenda asks for examples of the various ways people manage stress.

Submitted by Glenn Bannerman. This exercise is adapted from Bannerman and Fakkema, **Guide for Recreation Leaders**. *(Atlanta: John Knox Press).*

113 DEAR ME

Participants reflect on their needs, hopes and expectations as they write themselves a letter and share it with the group.

GOALS

To verbalize motivation for participation and articulate expectations for the learning experience.

GROUP SIZE

Unlimited.

TIME FRAME

10–15 minutes

MATERIALS

Dear Me worksheets for all.

PROCESS

☞ *Try **Dear Me P.S.**, p 112, as a companion closing process.*

1) The trainer distributes **Dear Me** worksheets and invites everyone to focus on their reasons for participating and their hopes for the learning experience.

   Participants are instructed to compose a letter to themselves by answering the questions in whatever way makes sense to them.

2) As soon as most people are finished, the trainer invites participants to introduce themselves by name and share one paragraph from their letter.

VARIATIONS

■ Divide into small groups (3–8 people) for the introductions and sharing in *Step 2*. If time permits, encourage participants to share their entire letters.

*This process is adapted from Read, Simon and Goodman, **Health Education: A Search for Values** (Englewood Cliffs NJ: Prentice-Hall, 1977). Available from Sagamore Bookstore, Racquette Lake NY 13436.*

Date:

DEAR ME:

What are my reasons for taking this course?

What special concerns, issues, questions would I like to see included?

What do I hope to learn here?

What do I not want?

What do I hope to accomplish with what I learn here?

Sincerely,

114 WANTED POSTERS

In this mysterious introduction process participants disclose the stress management *modus operandi* that elevated them to the FBI's *Most Wanted List.*

GOALS

To reflect on personal styles of managing stress.

To get acquainted.

GROUP SIZE

Unlimited as long as the room offers ample space for groups of four and eight to gather comfortably.

TIME FRAME

15–20 minutes

MATERIALS

Wanted Poster worksheets for all; Polaroid camera and film for variation.

PROCESS

1) The trainer announces that the FBI (Federal Bureau of Introductions) has put everyone in the group on the *Most Wanted List* and needs some personal data to include on their *Wanted Posters.*

2) **Wanted Posters** are distributed to all participants and the trainer guides the group through the process of completing the worksheet.

   ☞ *Pace your instructions so that most people are finished with one step before you announce the next.*

   ➤ First, write your vital statistics—name, birthplace and occupation.

   ➤ Next, draw features on the "mug shot" to reflect your mood today.

   ➤ Then fill in the next three blanks of the worksheet.
   - ➢ What are some of the situations that trigger your stress response?
   - ➢ What is your *modus operandi* (basic style of attack) in managing your stress? How do you typically cope?
   - ➢ What questionable coping techniques (eg, alcohol, withdrawal, cynicism, overeating) do you use regularly or occasionally?

➤ Use the caution list at the bottom of the worksheet to check the descriptions that apply to you.

3) The trainer invites participants to pair up with someone they don't know and introduce themselves by sharing vital statistics and their responses to the **Wanted** statements. (3 minutes)

4) After about three minutes the trainer interrupts and directs the dyads to find another twosome and make a quartet. After everyone is settled, participants are instructed to introduce themselves again, this time describing their "mug shots" and explaining their choice of cautions from the checklist.

5) The trainer reconvenes the group, solicits brief observations from participants and uses these comments as a bridge to the next content segment.

VARIATIONS

■ Take Polaroid photos of everyone as they arrive (or as they are filling out their **Wanted Posters**). At the end of the exercise participants attach their photos to their posters and display them for all to see.

■ After completing their in *Step 2*, participants are instructed to turn them over and jot down a few words about what they want from this learning experience. After *Step 4*, each foursome joins with another to make groups of eight where participants introduce themselves again, this time sharing some of their hopes and expectations.

W A N T E D

VITAL STATISTICS

_____

name

_____

birthplace

_____

occupation

WANTED for experiencing stress when . . .

WANTED for responding to stress by . . .

WANTED for using questionable copers such as . . .

CAUTION: This person is

____ wild and crazy   ____ scattered in many directions

____ harmless   ____ AWOL from work for a day

____ a ticking bomb   ____ known to be very responsible

____ on the run   ____ in hot pursuit of the meaning of life

____ on probation   ____ not guilty by reason of insanity

____ hard to pin down   ____ about to snap someone's head off

____ clever   ____ hazardous to his/her health

____ intense   ____ DWI (driven with imagination)

____ armed with great personal strength

____ wanted in several states of consciousness

____ other _____

Stress
Assessments

115 STRESS SPIDER WEB

This right-brain assessment helps participants articulate the sources of their stress and the accompanying thoughts, feelings and consequences.

GOALS

To clarify the meaning of stress.

To identify lifestyle sources of stress.

To explore feelings related to stress.

GROUP SIZE

Described for a group of 6–24 participants; could be adapted for larger groups.

TIME FRAME

20–30 minutes

MATERIALS

Stress Spider Web worksheets for all participants; blackboard or newsprint.

PROCESS

1) The trainer announces that participants will spend the next half hour exploring the meaning of stress—and how it applies to their lives.

2) She distributes **Stress Spider Web** worksheets and invites participants to begin free associating about stress and jotting down whatever thoughts and feelings come to mind as they ponder the following questions.

> ☞ *Stop after each instruction and allow plenty of time (2–3 minutes) for individuals to generate several responses and write them on their worksheets.*
>
> *The value of the exercise lies in the richness of examples that people produce. If necessary, try some group brainstorming in each area (definitions of stress, stressors and feelings) before asking participants to identify their own.*

➤ What does stress mean to you?

➤ Use the longer threads of the spider web to write down some of your *thoughts about stress and how you might define it.* For example, "stress is pressure," or "most of my stress is out of my control," or "stress is my response to demands."

☞ *Remind participants that there are no right answers. The spider web is just a tool to help us articulate our ideas and vague notions. You might say something like: "Don't worry about filling all the strands—hopefully this learning experience will help us all expand our understanding and sharpen our awareness of stress—so leave some room to grow! On the other hand, feel free to add more strands if you need to."*

➤ When you think about stress in your life, what images, experiences, situations, times, places, people come to mind (eg, planning meals and grocery shopping, poor performance, too much work to do, feeling empty, arguments, etc)?

➤ Jot down several specific *stressors* that cause you trouble at home or work. Use the *connecting strands of the web* to record some of your life stresses. (2–3 minutes)

➤ Now concentrate for a moment on the *feelings* you associate with stress (eg, anger, panic, discouragement, exhilaration, fatigue, etc) and jot them down wherever there is space on the web.

3) Participants are directed to form groups of three by finding two other people who recorded at least one stress-related feeling similar to one they listed.

The trainer instructs trios to spend 6 minutes (2 minutes apiece) sharing their definitions of stress, the stressors they experience and associated feelings.

☞ *Encourage people to add to their webs during this process as their neighbors' insights trigger memories or associations. This is a learning time—not a competition.*

4) After 6–8 minutes, the trainer interrupts the small groups. Participants are instructed to turn their worksheets over and answer the following questions as posed by the trainer.

➤ As you look over your stress spider web, what stands out for you as most significant? What association was most inclusive or most enlightening?

➤ What insights about stress did you gain in constructing your web and discussing it with your neighbors?

☞ *To help participants focus on specific details, ask them to complete a few of the following sentence stems appropriate to the remainder of your agenda:*

I learned . . .   I rediscovered . . .
I noticed . . .   I was pleased that . . .
I was surprised . . .   I hope that . . .
I wonder . . .   I want to learn more about . . .

5) The trainer invites participants to share their responses with the whole group. As people volunteer their insights and priorities, the trainer responds affirmatively to each and records them on newsprint.

6) After all have shared, the trainer surveys the issues raised. She highlights the themes that have surfaced and uses this information as a bridge to agenda-setting or an in-depth presentation on stress.

VARIATIONS

■ To use this exercise as an icebreaker, ask participants to list their hopes and expectations as part of *Step 2*. Invite people to pair up and discuss what they discovered (5 min), then introduce themselves to the group by sharing one or two expectations.

■ In larger groups, participants could form sextets for the sharing in *Step 5*. A recorder is appointed in each group and reports themes to the whole group in *Step 6*.

■ The same de-mystifying and clarifying spider web process could be used effectively with other fuzzy topics such as conflict, harassment, wellness, problem-solving, etc.

The inspiration for this exercise came from the "de-fuzzing wheel" of Don Read, Joel Goodman and Sid Simon in **Health Education: The Search for Values** *(Englewood Cliffs NJ: Prentice-Hall, 1977).*

STRESS SPIDER WEB

116 BODY MAPPING

In this life-size stress assessment participants mentally scan their body for tension, then pair up to map sources of physical stress.

GOALS

To identify areas of the body signaling physical stress.

To expand awareness of interventions for reducing physical stress.

GROUP SIZE

Unlimited.

TIME FRAME

30–45 minutes for groups of 20–25 people.

MATERIALS

Two eight-foot lengths of butcher paper for each participant; colored markers for each pair; carpeted room of adequate size for people to make life-size posters on the floor.

PROCESS

1) The trainer begins the exercise with a few comments on the nature of physical stress.

● The landscape of today's life and lifestyle are strewn with a great many stressors that linger for varying lengths of time. Some pressures (eg, work, marital problems, financial difficulties) may drag on indefinitely. Other tension sources (eg, a traffic jam, lost car keys, being late for an appointment) generate more casual or transitory problems. **Both immediate and long-term pressures can produce physical stress.**

● Psychological and behavioral factors play very important roles in governing our physical well-being. In fact, **there is a link between people's stress level and their frequency of physical illness.**

● An important first step in responding positively to debilitating stress is to recognize the symptoms—to be aware of stressors that manifest themselves in perceivable physical tension.

- **Many people are not aware of the presence and location of physical stress within their bodies.** Certain stress areas have been present for so long we simply get used to them. Some transitory tensions come and go without notice. Yet it is important to become aware of physical stress locations so we can initiate appropriate interventions to counteract the harmful side effects of that tension.

- Meditation, relaxation, mental imagery, pain management and exercise programs can effectively alleviate physical stress—but not unless we recognize when we need these tension antidotes.

2) The trainer invites participants to stand and find a partner who will help them map out their physical stress points.

3) As participants are finding partners, the trainer distributes markers and 4 sheets of butcher paper (3' x 8') to each pair and encourages them to spread out around the room. Once everyone is ready, he outlines the body-mapping process.

> ➤ You will take turns making an outline of your body (front and back views) and mapping the areas where you notice tension.

4) The trainer then leads the pairs through the first phase of the body mapping process, making front view body outlines.

> ☞ *This can cause some initial discomfort and anxiety for some. Encourage people to relax and pay attention to the physical messages they receive during this first step.*

> ➤ First, decide who is the *Elbow* and who is the *Knee*.

> ➤ Spread out one of your sheets of paper on the floor. *Elbows* should lie on their backs, centered on the paper while *Knees* use a marker to make a rough outline of their partner's body on the paper.

> > ➤ *Elbows:* Angle your arms away from your body and spread out your hands, palm up. Place your heels about 18 inches apart and let your toes turn out so that your partner can outline your foot.

> > ➤ *Knees:* Outline your partner's body—completely, but discreetly. Label the map *Front View*.

> ➤ Now switch roles. *Knees* lie down on a new sheet of paper, spread your arms and legs while your *Elbow* partner draws your body outline and marks it a *Front View*.

5) As soon as everybody has completed the body outline, the trainer announces that participants will spend the next few minutes getting in

touch with their physical stress and tension spots and leads them through a body-scanning sequence.

☞ *For maximum benefit to participants, allow plenty of time for the mental body scan for tension.*

➤ Everyone please lie down face up on your *Front View* body outline. Relax as much as possible. Take a few deep breaths and turn your attention inside your body.

➤ Mentally scan the front part of your body for tension, noticing any areas of tightness or discomfort. Scan the front of your body: from forehead to jaw; from neck and throat to chest; arms, hands, fingers; belly, hips, groin; thighs, shins, feet and toes. Don't hurry. Pay attention to the tension you feel.

Where on the front side of your body are you aware of physical stress or tension?

Can you tell which tension spots are chronic and which are transitory?

6) The trainer invites participants to record their discoveries on the body map.

➤ Now it's time to map the physical stress points you discovered. Take a few seconds to stretch and move around. Then grab some markers and draw on your body outline *Front View* all the areas of tension that you noticed.

➤ Shade in any area where you noticed stress or tension. The more stress or tension you felt, the darker you should shade the area. You may want to use a second color or some other symbol to distinguish chronic stress spots from transitory tension areas.

➤ You will have about 2 minutes to make your map. As you draw, feel free to describe what you discovered to your partner.

7) After 2–3 minutes the trainer interrupts and announces that many people experience significant stress and tension on the backside of their bodies, too! He invites everyone to make another body map and guides the group through *Steps 4, 5* and *6* again, this time lying face down on a new sheet of paper and scanning the backside of the body for tension.

☞ *Allow plenty of time for the body scan: beginning with the top of the scalp, down to the base of the skull and back of the neck; across the tops of the shoulders and between the shoulder blades; down the upper arms, elbows, forearms, wrists, hands; in the waist and lower back; hips and buttocks; back of thighs and knees, calves; heels, bottoms of feet, toes.*

---

8) After the *Back View* body maps are completed, the trainer directs partners to share their maps and describe their physical tension spots in detail, including any insights about sources of that stress.

9) The trainer interrupts after 3–4 minutes and suggests that participants take a few more minutes and exchange ideas with their partners about possible strategies for alleviating tension at some of their physical stress points.

10) After 3–5 minutes the trainer reconvenes the group and asks for examples of where people found tension in their bodies. If there seem to be some "favorite" spots (eg, lower back, toes, jaw, etc), the group can brainstorm suggestions for relieving tension in those areas.

VARIATIONS

■ As part of *Step 8*, participants with similar stress hot spots (eg, shoulders, stomach, eyes) could gather and discuss strategies for counteracting the effects of physical stress in that area of the body. To add a little spice, these body part groups could be asked to make up a country-western song title that expresses the unique misery of tension in that area. (eg, "Ever Since I Knowed You, Honey, You Been a Pain in the Neck to Me.")

■ A worksheet showing generic male and female front and back body outlines can be substituted for the life-sized body maps. After the body scan, participants can then shade in locations of physical stress they experienced.

■ The trainer could post two enlarged body outlines (front and back) and ask participants to record their individual physical stress spots on these group body maps. Discussion can be directed towards high density tension areas and possible interventions to help reduce these sources of physical stress.

Submitted by Kent Beeler.

117 ON THE JOB STRESS GRID

Participants use a special grid to pinpoint their job stress and its sources, then rank the intensity of their stress, identify their job "hot spots" and explore possibilities for coping.

GOALS

To identify the variety and intensity of vocation-related stressors.

To seek methods of coping with job-related "hot spots" that could lead to burnout.

GROUP SIZE

Unlimited.

TIME FRAME

25–40 minutes

MATERIALS

Blackboard or newsprint easel; **On the Job Stress Grid** and **On the Job Stress Analysis** worksheets for all participants.

PROCESS

1) The trainer introduces the exercise by outlining some or all of the following points about job stress.

- It is safe to say that everyone who has a job experiences **job-related stress**. Responsibility without authority, boring meetings, power struggles, office gossip, staff turnover, repetitive tasks, personality clashes—the work place is a fertile breeding ground for stress.

- Most people focus their attention on one or two irritants on the job, and overlook some of the less visible causes of stress. If your job is getting under your skin, take a look at the three major sources of stress—and satisfaction—on the job: *relationships, environment and job expectations.*

- **Relationships**. Contact with others at work can be one of our prime sources of job satisfaction. But relationships generate wearing distress when there is uncomfortable tension or unresolved conflict. Some studies indicate that interpersonal difficulty (with superiors, subordinates, peers or clients) is the primary source of work-related stress.

- **Environment.** Many of us work in a stressful physical environment. Noise, smoke, crowded conditions, poor ventilation, lack of windows, uncomfortable temperature or furniture—all can cause fatigue and tension. So can the "corporate culture." The organization's structure, policies, informal channels of influence, office politics and support networks all affect the quality of work life.

- **Job Expectations.** The nitty-gritty aspects of a job may be a major source of distress. When a person's skills are not well matched with the responsibilities of the job, stress and a gnawing feeling of inadequacy may result. Frustration mounts when the schedule becomes too hectic, or the work-load too great. Fuzzy job descriptions create ambiguity, uncertainty and anxiety. Financial and other rewards may be a source of despair.

- Clearly no job or work setting is perfect. Every job has a "crap factor." None is without varying degrees of frustration and stress. However, those people who are able to identify both the nature and source of this distress are in the best position to minimize the accumulation of stress on the job.

2) The trainer enlists the group's support in brainstorming a list of job stressors in each of the three categories: ***Relationships, Environment*** (physical and situational) and ***Job Expectations.***

   ☞ *Record every suggestion on the blackboard or newsprint.*

   Encourage participants to suggest a wide variety of specific stressors in each category. This idea generation will help people warm up to the task of completing their worksheet in the next phase.

   If the group totally misses a major aspect of one category, you may wish to direct their thinking by asking a facilitative question or by making additional suggestions.

3) The trainer distributes a copy of the **On the Job Stress Grid** to each participant and gives the following instructions.

   ➤ First, just look the grid over carefully. Notice that the three horizontal rows designate the type of stress (*Relationships, Environment* or *Job Expectations*). Each box in the row indicates a subcategory of that potential source of stress.

   ➤ As you scan the grid, consider the various types of stress you experience on the job (eg, balky computer, grouchy neighbor, bad pay, too much overtime, over-critical supervisor, lazy staff, tiny office, customer complaints, etc) and list each stressor in the proper box.

➣ Be as specific as possible. List as many stresses as possible in the time allowed. The more detailed your grid, the more helpful it will be to you. But there's no need to write an essay. A word or two will do.

➣ List more than one stressor in some boxes if it seems appropriate.

Don't worry about putting something in every box. Use the category to jar your memory, list those stresses that apply and move on. Some boxes will probably remain empty.

➣ Some stressors may fit in several places. Feel free to list them more than once.

☞ *Pause about 5 minutes here so that participants can complete the grid. You may need to clarify instructions for some. The idea is to get as complete a picture as possible of the wide variety of stresses that people experience on the job.*

➤ Stop and mentally step back from the details of your grid and look again at the overall box categories (eg, *Authorities, Subordinates, Office Politics, Schedule, Rewards,* etc). Notice the clustering of your stressors in the 12 categories.

➤ Now, for each category box, consider the intensity of the stress you experience and rate the intensity using the 0–5 scale on the bottom of the grid.

0 = Not at all stressful   *3 = Moderately stressful*
1 = Minimally stressful   *4 = Quite stressful*
2 = Somewhat stressful   *5 = Extremely stressful*

➤ Write your rating for each category in the smaller inset box.

➤ Total your score for each column and record your total *relationship, environment* and *job expectations* scores on the bottom of the worksheet. Then calculate your overall score.

➤ Take a minute or two to reflect on your grid and record your observations at the bottom of the worksheet.

4) The trainer distributes **On the Job Stress Analysis** worksheets to all and instructs participants to spend a few minutes reflecting on their job stress grids and then answer the questions on the **Analysis** worksheet.

5) The trainer divides participants into groups of 4–5 members each or utilizes previously established discussion units. Participants are invited to discuss their observations and discoveries about on-the-job stress with one another, using their worksheet grids as the basis for sharing. (20 minutes; 4–5 minutes each)

> ☞ *If this session is being conducted for a group of people who work together, caution participants to be discreet. Humor can be disarming: "If your boss is in your group and you've listed your boss all over your grid, cover it up and lie!"*

6) The trainer reconvenes the entire group and invites the brief sharing of observations and insights.

7) The trainer asks participants to scan their worksheets once again and to identify the areas of greatest current tension—their *job stress hot spots!* Participants are instructed to circle the hot spots on their grid.

8) The trainer briefly outlines three basic coping options for job stress and asks participants to consider which of these options would best help them cool down one of their hot spots.

- **Take a recess**. Get out of the stress for awhile. Take a break. Do something else. Take a walk, go out to dinner, tackle a home project, listen to music, exercise, etc. Don't worry—your hot spot will still be there when you get back, the same as it was before. But you will be different after you take a break.

- **Identify your stress-creating habits**. Ask yourself whether you're keeping your hot spot hot by being a perfectionist or being in such a hurry, by worrying too much or trying to control everything, by exaggerating or ignoring things? Are you making matters worse?

- **Examine your job stress**. Can you *eliminate* or ignore it? If not, can you *modify* it in some way that will cool it down a bit? If not, can you admit that it's out of your control and *make peace with it*, let it carry you along for the ride? After all, if you simply can't fight it, then you're smarter to "go with the flow."

9) The trainer invites participants to select the coping option that seems most relevant for their personal hot spot and experiment with giving it a try and observing the results.

VARIATIONS

■ As part of *Step 3* the trainer may present an objective scoring system for the **Job Stress Grid**:

0–19 You must work in a model work environment, or stagnation may be just around the corner. You may need a little more stress to keep your job interesting.

20–35 Apparently your job offers you enough challenge to keep you interested, growing and on your toes. If specific stressors cause you difficulty, you should have the energy and perspective to deal with them.

36–50 You are the only one who knows how much stress stimulates you without wearing you out. With this score you might want to take a second look at your job stressors and work toward changing the ones that drain you.

51–60 You may be paying a high price for your high stress work habits. This job could be a killer for you.

☞ *This is not a standardized test, so use the scoring system with sensitivity and a sense of humor. Obviously participants' scores will go up or down depending on the number of stressors they could think of. This is likely to be as much a function of the time allowed to complete the grid and the creativity level of the group as it is of job-related stress.*

■ As part of *Step 3* the trainer could challenge the group to create their own scoring system. By asking people to stand and indicate their score level (eg, 0–10, 11–20, etc), a group "curve" can be observed and used for comparison.

☞ *This strategy is only for groups where a fair degree of anonymity can be guaranteed. In smaller or more intimate groups it may put pressure on some people to reveal what they would rather keep to themselves.*

■ At the end of *Step 6* the trainer could generate a group profile of "hot spot" patterns. Recreate the worksheet grid on the blackboard or newsprint. Fill in the category location for each participant's hot spot. Then ask the group for comments and observations on the "mini-study" they have just completed in constructing their group profile.

ON THE JOB STRESS GRID

INTENSITY RATING		
0 = Not at all stressful 1 = Minimally stressful	2 = Somewhat stressful 3 = Moderately stressful	4 = Quite stressful 5 = Overwhelmingly stressful
JOB EXPECTATIONS	**ENVIRONMENT**	**RELATIONSHIPS**
job requirements/ activities/description	physical environment	with authorities (boss, supervisor)
workload	organizational climate	with subordinates
schedule	power dynamics office politics	with peers, colleagues
financial compensation non-monetary rewards	support systems recognition	with clients, customers
JOB EXPECTATIONS TOTAL _____	ENVIRONMENT TOTAL _____	RELATIONSHIPS TOTAL _____

TOTAL OVERALL _____

ON THE JOB STRESS ANALYSIS

EVALUATION

I believe that my overall score is

_____ too high   _____ just right   _____ too low

I believe that my overall score is

_____ higher than other peoples'

_____ about average/normal

_____ lower than most others'

OBSERVATIONS

I experience most stress on the job with

_____ relationships   _____ environment   _____ job expectations

I have the least stress in my job with

_____ relationships   _____ environment   _____ job expectations

REFLECTIONS

I am surprised that . . .

I discovered . . .

OBSERVATIONS

My job "hot spots" are:

TRAINER'S NOTES

118 STRESS ATTITUDES SURVEY

Participants use their feet and heads to express and explore attitudes toward stress in this human values continuum.

GOALS

To raise consciousness about personal beliefs related to stress.

To re-evaluate and articulate attitudes toward stress.

To promote group interaction and involvement.

GROUP SIZE

Works best with 12–30 people, but can be adapted for smaller and larger groups.

TIME FRAME

20–30 minutes

MATERIALS

Three newsprint easels (or several sheets with tape for each of the three "positions") and markers.

PROCESS

1) The trainer announces that during the next half hour participants will have an opportunity to dramatically express their opinions and attitudes about stress by indicating whether they agree with, disagree with, or remain neutral toward a series of statements.

   ☞ *To warm up the group, you could use one or two of the statements here as voting questions.* ***How many agree? Disagree? Neutral?***

2) The trainer designates a spot on one side of the room to represent the position *I agree* and an area on the opposite side to represent *I disagree*. She indicates a midpoint between these two positions and labels it *Neutral*.

   ☞ *Place a newsprint easel and markers at each location. It's helpful to prepare the newsprint in advance with the position (agree, disagree, neutral) printed on the top sheet and the statements you plan to use in the next step written at the top of the underlying*

sheets. Use one sheet per question and leave space for partici-
pants to write. Leave an extra blank sheet between statements in
case you have a profile group.

3) The trainer reads one of the **Stress Attitude Statements** and instructs
   participants to stand up and move to the position in the room that
   represents their personal position (agree, disagree, neutral) in response
   to this issue.

   ☞ *You may want to "rehearse" this step once or twice with different*
   statements and practice moving before proceeding to discussion
   in the next step.

4) As soon as everyone has taken a position, the trainer gives instructions
   for each group.

   ➤ The *agree* group should discuss reasons why you agree with the
   statement.

   ➤ On the newsprint record all the ideas and examples that
   substantiate that position. Leave space at the bottom.

   ➤ When you've run out of ideas, together revise the original
   statement in a way that strengthens it and your commitment to
   the position.

   ➤ Write the final version of your statement at the bottom of your
   newsprint.

   ➤ The *disagree* group should brainstorm why you disagree with the
   statement.

   ➤ Record your objections on the newsprint, but leave room at the
   bottom.

   ➤ When you've exhausted your dissent, revise the original statement so that you can all agree with it.

   ➤ Write the new form at the bottom.

   ➤ The *neutral* group should divide your newsprint in half.

   ➤ On one side list all the ways in which you agree with the
   statement. On the other side, list your disagreements.

   ➤ Then see if your can revise the statement so you all agree with
   it.

   ➤ Write down your best version.

   ➤ You will have 5 minutes to complete the task.

   ☞ *If there is only one person at any position, encourage him*
   either to stick to his guns and complete the task alone, or to

> *join one of the other groups and lobby for his position in revising the statements.*

5) After 5 minutes the trainer calls time and asks for a brief report from each group.

6) The three newsprint statements are collected and posted at the front of the room. *Steps 4* and *5* are repeated several times using a new statement each time.

7) The trainer summarizes the group's attitudes as reflected in the posters and makes a few comments on the importance of personal beliefs and attitudes as shapers of our responses to stress.

TRAINER'S NOTES

Based on a human decision continuum exercise submitted by Sandy Queen.

©1994 Whole Person Press 210 W Michigan Duluth MN 55802   (800) 247-6789

STRESS ATTITUDE STATEMENTS

■ Stress is hazardous to your health.

■ Our times are more stressful than previous eras.

■ Kids should be protected from stressful situations.

■ Relaxation techniques are a waste of time.

■ I am responsible for all my stress and its effect on me because I choose my reactions and responses.

■ Anxiety is a normal response to stress.

■ People use stress as an excuse not to take responsibility for things.

■ 99% of stress is caused between our ears.

■ Everyday hassles cause just as much stress as big things like divorce or unemployment.

■ Some people are immune to stress.

■ It's okay to take tranquilizers when you're under a lot of stress that you can't control.

■ Stress can be good for you.

■ Coping effectively early in life provides protection against stress and builds resistance to it later in life.

■ Watching TV is a great way to manage stress.

■ One person's stressors are another person's challenge.

■ Some people are more vulnerable to stress than others.

■ The best way to manage stress is to learn how to relax.

■ A sedentary lifestyle lowers our resistance to stress.

■ As far as stress is concerned, your imagination is your own worst enemy.

■ Sitting down with a drink is a good way to unwind.

■ Relationships are the biggest source of stress for most people.

■ Every bad feeling you have is the result of your distorted thinking.

119 STRESS SKETCH

In this imaginative stress assessment, participants draw a major life stress and engage it in a provocative conversation.

GOALS

To explore in depth the mind/body/spirit dimensions of a major life struggle.

To encourage non-linear approaches to stress management.

To affirm individuals' capacity for insight into the source and impact of stress in their lives.

GROUP SIZE

Unlimited if there is plenty of room to spread out and hard surfaces for drawing; works well with individuals.

TIME FRAME

30–40 minutes

MATERIALS

Two sheets of unlined paper for all participants; crayons, fineline markers, colored pencils or pens for everyone; oversize paper or newsprint is fun to use if there is space.

PROCESS

☞ *This assumes that participants are warmed up to the subject of stress and have developed some degree of trust through previous self-disclosure in small groups.*

1) The trainer distributes paper and drawing materials to participants and announces that during the next half hour they will be exploring a major life stress in depth. She invites people to turn their focus inward, then guides them through the process of choosing a life challenge to investigate.

   ➤ Think about the major stress or problem in your life right now. Perhaps it's a deteriorating relationship or a house full of toddlers or a demanding new job or an unexpected financial burden or a home improvement project or even a midlife crisis. What is the key challenge you are facing today?

➤ Take a moment to get that challenge clearly in mind. Ask yourself, "What am I struggling with? What shape or form is it? Is it within me or outside? Is anyone else involved in the problem? How big is it?"

☞ *Don't rush. Allow silence and time for the images to develop. After a minute or two check to make sure that everyone has a specific stress, challenge, problem or struggle in mind.*

➤ Close your eyes and visualize your struggle. What images come to mind? Allow the images to come and go, to change and fade, to re-emerge. Pay attention to the faces of your struggle.

☞ *Give the next series of directions slowly and thoughtfully. Stop between each thought or image and allow plenty of space for the mental exploration process. To help gauge the pacing, try imaging your own struggle!*

➤ As the image of this challenge forms vividly in your mind, notice if you have any *physical* reactions or symptoms that seem to be related to your struggle . . . a heartache, for example, or an upset stomach, or a tight fist. Notice any physical sensations you experience as you mentally recall and relive your struggle.

➤ As you continue to picture this major source of stress in your life, notice if you have any *emotional* reactions. Do you feel worried or powerful or angry or apathetic? Allow the feelings to surface as you keep imaging the struggle.

➤ In the midst of your struggle notice any *spiritual* reactions that you might have. Does this problem challenge your values? Affirm them? Is there any special meaning here for you? Does the struggle touch the core of your being?

2) The trainer now interrupts the visualization process and instructs participants to *silently* draw their struggle, embellishing it with some representation of the physical, emotional and spiritual reactions they experienced while imaging their stress.

☞ *Encourage people to stay with the images they have just experienced and portray them pictorially on paper. Reassure skeptics that no one will be judging their artistic talents. You could say, "The point here is personal growth, not performance. Relax and allow yourself to explore drawing as a means to greater awareness and self-understanding."*

3) After about 5–7 minutes the trainer directs participants to give their drawings a name. Once everyone has a title, the trainer guides participants through a dialogue with their drawings.

> ➤ Look closely at your drawing and open yourself to learning from this graphic teacher.

> ➤ Let your drawing speak to you. Imagine what this picture of your struggle would say to you if it could talk.

> ☞ *Pause here.*

> ➤ Now respond. Take a sheet of blank paper and start writing down this conversation with your drawing as if it were a script for a play. Don't worry about grammar or spelling or logic. Just listen to what your drawing has to tell you and write it down. Then write down your answer and the drawing's response.

> ☞ *If some people have trouble staying on track, suggest that they focus on letting the drawing describe itself in words.*

4) After about 5 minutes the trainer regains the group's attention. She instructs people to rejoin their small groups and spend 10 minutes reading their conversations to one another and sharing what they discovered about stress and their body/mind/spirit reactions during this visualization, drawing and writing process.

5) After 10 minutes the trainer reconvenes the group and invites observations, reflections, or public reading of dialogues.

6) In conclusion, the trainer recommends that participants experiment with this technique when they feel particularly tense or worried.

> ● Drawing the problem and engaging it in dialogue can help you get to the heart of the problem and help get you on the path to confronting and resolving it.

VARIATIONS

■ With skittish audiences where the trust level is not high, skip the in *Step 4*. Instead, participants could pair up for sharing or the trainer could invite volunteers to read their conversations. Some brave soul is bound to get the ball rolling.

■ The data generated about physical, emotional and spiritual reactions could be pooled for group discussion on the whole person side effects of stress.

TRAINER'S NOTES

*Submitted by Lucia Capacchione. This process is adapted from her book, **The Creative Journal** (Athens OH: Ohio University Press, 1979).*

120 LIFETRAP 4: GOOD GRIEF?

In this powerful self-reflection and sharing exercise, participants explore loss as a common source of stress and grieving as a natural process of healing. They identify distressing symptoms of a personal loss, compare their experience with the typical stages of grief and explore methods for reducing the stress of grief.

GOALS

To recognize that while every loss causes distress, proper grieving leads toward healing.

To identify the normal stages of the grief process.

To foster healthful skills for coping with the pain of loss.

GROUP SIZE

Unlimited.

TIME FRAME

60–90 minutes

MATERIALS

Good Grief Cycle and **Observations** worksheets for all.

PROCESS

 This is a five-part exerciseon stress of grief:

A) *Opening chalktalk and optional reading. (5–10 minutes)*

B) *Personal reflection and exploration of the grief process using worksheets. (20–30 minutes)*

C) *Small group sharing. (20–25 minutes)*

D) *Large group discussion. (5–10 minutes)*

E) *Closing chalktalk and suggestions for coping. (10–15 minutes)*

A. Chalktalk (5-10 minutes)

1) The trainer introduces the exercise with the following comments about grief.

- **Change is inevitable.** Nothing is permanent. If you care about something or someone, one fact is certain: someday you will have to say "goodbye." Saying goodbye is always painful because you have lost a treasure. We are all scarred and wounded veterans of some loss.

- **Grief is universal** because grief results from the pain of loss—any loss. You may experience the empty, desperate feelings of grief with a divorce or the death of a loved one. But you also grieve the lesser losses of daily living—job changes, disappointments, disruptions in the family, altered friendships, unfulfilled dreams, or diminishing abilities.

- **Grief is not the problem, it's the solution!** Grief is the process of healing that follows any loss. It is natural and necessary. You don't cure grief, you heal through it. This healing proceeds through a series of predictable, natural stages.

- **When grief is viewed as something to be avoided, trouble may start.** Unrecognized, unhealed grief leaves festering wounds and is a causal factor in a surprising amount of stress-related disease. When you adopt coping methods designed to hide your feelings and numb your pain, you delay the process of healing. Unfinished grief is a powerful source of distress.

  ☞ *You may wish to read the **Mustard Seed** parable (p 127) to amplify these introductory comments.*

B. Worksheets (20–30 minutes)

2) The trainer distributes a copy of the **Good Grief Cycle** and **Observations** worksheets to participants and invites them to spend a few moments silently identifying some of the loss experiences.

  ➤ Recall several losses you have experienced *in the past* and some you are *currently grieving*. Record your losses in *Section A* of the worksheet.

  ☞ *Give several concrete examples representing a wide range of losses (eg, death of a pet, move to a new apartment, favorite TV show taken off the air, loss of play time because of increased job demands, changes in children as they develop, prolonged illness, empty nest, changed relationship, retirement, leaving school, fight with a best friend, loss of faith, declining physical prowess, etc).*

  You may also ask the group to brainstorm ideas together before focusing on their own specific recent losses.

3) The trainer asks participants to look over their list of losses.

> ➤ Choose one loss experience you would like to examine more closely for yourself. Write this grief-focus on the worksheet in *Section B.*

4) Once everyone has a specific loss in mind, the trainer describes the grief process, one stage at a time. Participants follow along, using their worksheets to record insights and observations about their loss as the trainer directs.

- ● *Stage 1: Shock.* Shock is the natural anesthesia of the human emotional system. When the pain is too great, our mental/emotional/ spiritual systems simply "blow a fuse" and can't process everything we experience. We shut down to protect ourselves from the pain. This shock often breeds denial. People say, "I just can't believe it!" and they may continue as if nothing has happened.
  - > ➤ In *Section C,* *circle* the elements of this stage (shock) that you have experienced with the loss you have chosen to examine.
  - > ➤ Then briefly describe your observations about this stage in *Section D.*

- ● *Stage 2: Pain.* When the self-protective anesthesia of shock wears off, people begin to experience the pain of the loss. Our systems start opening up. Emotions well up. We may feel angry, sad, scared. We feel lonely, depressed, panicky. We get physically sick.

  As painful as these feelings are, emotional turmoil is cleansing. It signals the next stage of healing through feeling. The gradual process of saying goodbye has begun. If feelings are shut down, the healing cannot continue.
  - > ➤ In *Section C,* *circle* the elements of this stage (pain) that you have experienced with the loss you have chosen as your focus.
  - > ➤ Then, in *Section D,* briefly describe your observations about this stage in your grief process.

- ● *Stage 3: Stuck.* As the constancy and intensity of the feelings begin to subside (after a few hours, or days, or after many months) people start trying to live a normal life again. Seldom is this easy. We experience frightening flashbacks and radical mood swings. We have trouble getting going. We wonder if something is wrong with us ("Am I crazy?"). We are often tired, withdrawn and depressed.

  Again, these feelings are a sign of gradual adaptation, the first steps to rebuilding a new life—as slow and as difficult as it may seem.
  - > ➤ Once again, in *Section C,* *circle* the symptoms of being "stuck" that you have experienced with your loss.

➤ Then record your observations of this stage in *Section D*.

● *Stage 4: Strength.* At some point, often unexpectedly, hope breaks through. Slowly, a new life is affirmed and people are able to say, "I've lost something, but I love life again." At this stage we no longer grit our teeth to get through the day. We begin to recommit ourselves and reach out.

Through pain we would never have chosen, we move to a deeper level of wisdom. We begin to understand the adage, *Life breaks everyone . . . and then some heal stronger at the broken places.* We begin to understand our new-found strengths and look for situations in which we can reach out and touch others with love.

➤ Look at the elements of strength in *Stage 4* on your worksheet. *Circle* those that you have experienced.

➤ Then briefly describe your experience of strengthening and wisdom in *Section D*.

5) The trainer points out that everyone heals through the grief process in their own individual manner. He invites participants to reflect on their style of grieving by filling out the **Observations** worksheet (*Sections E, F,* and *G*).

C. Small groups (20–25 minutes)

6) The trainer divides the participants into smaller groups of 4–5 people, or uses previously established discussion units. Participants are invited to share their personal grief experience with one another, using the following guidelines.

➤ Take 4–5 minutes each to share your grief experience. Take your time and share in depth, but only what seems appropriate to you.

➤ Describe to your group the loss on which you focused. Then share your observations of how you experienced or are now experiencing the process of grieving.

➤ Be sure, also, to share some of the strengths and depth you have now grown to know through this experience—or what you think you might learn later in the process.

➤ As you listen to the stories of others in your group, don't try to fix the pain or make them feel better. Don't worry about a few tears. Certainly don't give advice. Just listen and understand and show that you care.

D. Discussion (5–10 minutes)

7) The trainer reconvenes the entire group and asks for observations and reflections. If the following points do not emerge from the discussion, the trainer may wish to offer some or all of these thoughts for consideration.

- Grief is a natural result of loss. Grief is necessary. It helps you heal. The duration of grief corresponds to the depth of the loss.
- Grief affects the whole person: body, mind, spirit and relationships.
- People seldom experience the grief stages in exact sequence. Healing is herky-jerky. Distress occurs when people stop the healing process and get themselves stuck in one stage.
- While recalling your grief and sharing it with others, as you have just done, may be painful, sharing your grief with others is also one of the most powerful sources of healing.

E. Chalktalk (10–15 minutes)

8) In closing, the trainer offers several suggestions for coping with the stress of grief.

- **Give yourself permission to grieve.** When we undergo surgery we accept the fact that we won't regain full physical strength for quite some time. Often, however, when we experience emotional loss we don't give ourselves time to heal. We compound the problem by becoming impatient. You need to give yourself permission to feel the pain that follows loss. Time does heal—but time is not enough. You need to let yourself heal through the feelings and stages of grief.
- **Take care of yourself.** Eat well. Try to get enough sleep. Exercise moderately. Be gentle with yourself. Don't be in a big hurry. You need tender loving care! Give it to yourself!!
- **Lean on others.** Share your grief with others—it keeps the healing process flowing. Join a group of people who are each working through their own grief process and who are committed to caring. Sometimes you can't do it alone. Reach out. Ask for support. Ask for help.
- **Work on your faith.** Loss signals life's impermanence. Grief reminds us of death. Faith helps you deal with others' deaths as well as your own. Every grief experience invites you to renew your acquaintance with the mysteries of life and reclaim your faith stance according to your current wisdom and understanding.

- **Invest yourself again.** After you've been hurt, it's natural to turn inward and resist the risk of caring again. The healing process of grief, however, demands new commitments. Look for people and challenges in which you can reinvest your love and attention.
- **Capitalize on the strengths that result from grief.** Although grief is seldom an experience we choose, it is an opportunity for growth. As a result of your pain you will find new strengths. Use them to help yourself and others. Through pain you never volunteered for, you become more able to sing your own unique song of love. Sing it clearly!

TRAINER'S NOTES

GOOD GRIEF CYCLE

A1. Major grief experiences in my lifetime:	A2. Grief (loss) experiences I'm dealing with now:	B. My focus for examination

STAGES IN HEALING

loss ──────────── What are you in the process of letting go of? Healing from? How is it effecting you? ──────► **reaffirmation**

STAGE 1
shock

STAGE 2
pain

STAGE 3
stuck

STAGE 4
strengths

"I can't believe it!"

"I hurt!"

"I can't get going."

"I am stronger."

C. STAGE 1: SHOCK	STAGE 2: PAIN	STAGE 3: STUCK	STAGE 4: STRENGTHS
shock . . . numbness . . . disbelief . . . emptiness . . . disconnected . . . drained . . . spacey *"I know but I don't really know."* *"I feel but I don't really feel."* *"It's not true!"* denial, withdrawal	resentment . . . anger . . . bitterness . . . guilt . . . sadness . . . depression . . . loneliness . . . hurt . . . emptiness . . . confusion . . . panic . . . aching . . . hopeless . . . turmoil . . . terror *"No one understands!"* *"I am empty."* *"What did I do?"* weeping, preoccupation, physical symptoms	isolated . . . afraid . . . insecure . . . disorganized . . . lethargic . . . blue . . . exhausted . . . dispirited *"I must be crazy!"* *"I'm not normal"* Flashbacks, mood swings, unproductive, withdrawal	responsible . . . accepting . . . moments of hope . . . caring again *"I am recovering."* *"Life is worth living after all!"* recommitment, reaching out, involvement, helping someone, friendship, treasured memories, deeper understanding of spirit, trust, sharing self, laughter
D. *MY EXPERIENCE* *I . . .*	*MY EXPERIENCE* *I . . .*	*MY EXPERIENCE* *I . . .*	*MY EXPERIENCE* *I . . .*

GOOD GRIEF OBSERVATIONS

E. How would you describe your general pattern for handling loss experiences?

Generally, I . . .

F. Reflecting on the grief you have experienced recently (or over your lifetime), what strengths have you gained because of that grief?

I am . . .

I know . . .

I believe . . .

I understand . . .

G.How could you use these strengths to aid others?

I could . . .

I want to . . .

I might . . .

I will . . .

Management
Strategies

121 A GOOD STRESS MANAGER

In this two-stage exercise, participants brainstorm qualities and behaviors of effective stress managers, then in small groups compile their own coping assessment instruments and test themselves.

GOALS

To identify effective attitudes and approaches for managing stress.

To elicit and reinforce participants' internal wisdom.

To assess personal coping style.

GROUP SIZE

Described for 12–24 people, but can easily be modified for smaller or larger groups.

TIME FRAME

30–60 minutes

MATERIALS

Several sheets of blank paper and **A Good Stress Manager** worksheets for all (or *A Good Stress Manager* list previously generated by the group); newsprint, markers and masking tape for each small group.

☞ *This exercise is designed in two parts so that the participants' A Good Stress Manager lists generated in Step 2 can be collected and duplicated for distribution in Step 3. If this timing is not appropriate for your setting, use the A Good Stress Manager list on p 54 as a worksheet and invite participants to add their own ideas before moving on to the small group process in Step 3.*

PROCESS

1) The trainer introduces the general concept of successful stress management as a *management* issue, covering some or all of the following points and amplifying with personal examples.

   • **Human beings are intrinsically good stress managers.** Our bodies and psyches are marvelously designed to respond appropriately and creatively to the host of challenges that require daily response. We are flexible, adaptive, reasonable. We are by nature problem solvers.

- **There is no universal best way to manage stress.** Each of us has a unique history and personal style that affects how we cope. An approach that works for me may not work for you. Each stressful situation is also different and requires different management strategies. A strategy that works for managing the stress of giving a speech may not be effective for handling the strain of chronic illness or for teaching your teenager how to drive.

- **Everyone is an expert at managing stress.** In the crucible of our life experience each of us has learned a wide repertoire of behaviors, attitudes, approaches, responses, techniques and skills for coping. We usually take for granted this internal wisdom, even though it was gained at a great price.

- **People around us are a rich resource for consultation.** Stress management is usually a private process for most of us. We rarely talk about our struggles—or our successes—in managing stress. Because of our feelings of vulnerability or inadequacy we cut ourselves off from those around us who may have learned something different (and helpful!) about managing stress. What a pity!

2) The trainer announces that participants will have an opportunity to pool their wisdom about stress management and to evaluate themselves as stress managers.

   She distributes blank paper to participants and asks them to reflect on the qualities, attitudes or behaviors they believe contribute to effective stress management.

   ➤ This is an opportunity to tune in to your own internal wisdom. Complete the sentence *A good stress manager* . . . in at least 10 different ways.

   ☞ *Give several examples (eg, "A good stress manager worries wisely," or "A good stress manager looks for alternatives," or "A good stress manager never eats to cope," etc).*

   ➤ Don't labor over the project. The first thing that pops into your head is likely to provoke surprising insights. Just write as fast as you can whatever comes to mind.

3) The trainer collects everyone's lists and announces that all statements will be compiled into an anonymous list of all definitions to be used at a later meeting.

4) At a later time, the trainer distributes the **A Good Stress Manager** list. Participants are directed to read through the list, marking as they go any statement that tickles their fancy.

☞ *If you are substituting the **A Good Stress Manager** worksheet on p 54, solicit additions from the group before moving on to **Step 5**.*

5) After everyone has finished marking their lists, the trainer invites participants to rejoin previous sharing groups, or forms new groups of 4 people.

☞ *To form new groups, ask people to find 3 others in the room who marked **at least one** of the same statements as intriguing. Groups should find a comfortable and fairly private space to work together (tables are nice!).*

6) As soon as the groups are settled, the trainer gives instructions for the development of do-it-yourself stress assessments.

➤ As a group, your job during the next 15 minutes is to develop a simple stress test, using items you chose from the **A Good Stress Manager** list and a scoring system your group devises together.

➤ Assume that this simple stress management test will be used in a learning situation to help people focus on and assess their stress management styles.

➤ You may select up to 10 statements to include in your assessment instrument. Feel free to add a few new phrases of your own.

➤ Decide on a format for your instrument. The approach for answering should be the same for all items. Examples:
  ➣ *True/False;*
  ➣ *Strongly Agree, Agree, Uncertain, Disagree, Strongly Disagree;*
  ➣ *1–10 scale;*
  ➣ *Describes me: Frequently . . . Sometimes;*
  ➣ *Letter grade for effort or performance.*

7) After 5–10 minutes the trainer circulates among the groups, distributing newsprint, markers and masking tape and giving the next instructions quietly to each different group.

➤ Once you have decided on your test items and scoring system, your next task is to transfer your assessment to newsprint. Write legibly and large enough so that it can be seen at a distance, but try to make it fit on two newsprint sheets.

➤ Choose a name for your test and write it at the top of the poster.

➤ Then use a third newsprint sheet to make a scoring key for your instrument that is self-explanatory and easy to read.

8) Five minutes before the end of the test development period, the trainer notifies groups and exhorts them to get their instruments down on paper and up on the wall.

9) The trainer invites participants to assess their stress management styles, using the instruments developed by the collective wisdom of the groups.

➤ Each group should begin in front of its own poster.

➤ Use a blank sheet of paper to record the name of the instrument. Then take the test using the accompanying scoring system and record your score and interpretation.

☞ *You may want to make an announcement for compulsive notetakers: "Don't copy all the items—just take the test and score yourself! The tests will be duplicated and handed out later!"*

➤ I will call time in about 2 minutes. All groups will then move clockwise around the room to the next poster/instrument and repeat the test-taking process.

➤ Eventually you will try all the assessments. You may want to jot down any surprises, insights, disappointments, reservations, or questions that you have along the way.

☞ *You will need to keep this process moving quickly, especially if scoring systems are complicated. Encourage estimating and extrapolating as necessary. If the energy of the group starts to flag, stop after three or four self-tests.*

10) After participants have completed several self-tests, the trainer re-convenes the large groups and asks participants to reflect on several questions.

☞ *Make sure that the discussion focuses not only on evaluation of the instruments, but also on what participants learned about themselves!*

✔ What did you learn about yourself as a stress manager?

✔ What themes recurred?

✔ How did the instruments compare in content and scoring?

✔ How well do you think these self-tests assess stress management capabilities and behaviors?

11) The trainer facilitates discussion of these issues and others that arise, then summarizes the learnings.

VARIATION

■ After *Step 10*, participants rejoin the original group and share insights learned during the exercise.

■ The trainer can duplicate all instruments and distribute copies of each to participants at a later date.

TRAINERS NOTES

*Thanks to Gloria Singer for contributions to the **A Good Stress Manager** list.*

©1994 Whole Person Press 210 W Michigan Duluth MN 55802   (800) 247-6789

A GOOD STRESS MANAGER . . .

- knows for herself how much challenge, pressure, stimulation is enough and how much is too much
- avoids potentially stressful situations
- dreams of becoming an Olympic champion
- nips stress in the bud
- understands that she is not indispensable
- never eats to cope
- never eats his heart out
- never chews someone else out
- believes that other people have good ideas, valuable skills and a basic willingness to do what needs to be done
- never worries
- smiles inside and lets go when starting to feel frantic
- sets appropriate goals and priorities
- sees challenges rather than problems
- knows when to say NO
- knows when to say YES
- feels genuinely connected to others
- can enjoy solitude
- remembers that he will die someday—and chooses wisely every moment
- has positive self-esteem
- doesn't blame herself or anyone else
- has patience
- backs off occasionally
- takes time to see, hear, smell and touch
- depends on his support network
- is optimistic
- can take disappointment in stride
- lightens up and plays when the going gets tough
- has drive
- practices saying "I'm sorry, I made a mistake"
- is a good problem solver
- takes care of herself

■ looks for a better idea
■ can have fun without spending money
■ can spend money without feeling guilty
■ sleeps on it
■ takes care of herself
■ doesn't get upset about little things
■ never uses TV as an escape
■ uses TV as an escape
■ breaks the big jobs into easy little tasks
■ finds satisfaction in working hard for something she wants
■ lets the feelings be—and then watches them change
■ understands that she is not perfect
■ remembers to express gratitude and appreciation to others
■ picks his fights carefully . . . and lets the little ones go
■ has a vision for herself and her world, and works to achieve it
■ has and continually develops a value and spiritual belief system
■ responds in proportion to the situation
■ is flexible in body, mind and spirit
■ pays attention to physical tension and knows how to relax
■ eats regular, well-balanced meals
■ cares about and practices physical fitness
■ knows how to pace herself
■ feels worthwhile, important and in charge of his life
■ knows the difference between stress that challenges and stress
   that threatens
■ sits quietly and thinks
■ spends minimal time dwelling on resentments, grudges and
   jealousies
■ asks himself, "50 years from now, who will know or care?"
■ can say HELP and accept it when it's offered
■ shares his heart with another and asks for feedback
■ values curiosity, imagination and humor in self and others
■ is flexible enough to respond to any crisis appropriately
■ has lots of different coping skills
■ manages time well

122 OBLIGATION OVERLOAD

Participants envision reducing their stress by eliminating specific obligations, then in practice standing up to internal and external pressures that make such a change difficult.

GOALS

To understand the many factors that keep us over-committed.

To practice standing up to pressure from outside and pressure from within when attempting to make a change.

To appreciate that other people go through the same kind of turmoil we do when trying to reduce their obligations.

GROUP SIZE

Unlimited.

TIME FRAME

45 minutes

PROCESS

☞ *Try the **Merry-Go-Round** energizer, p 122, as a warm-up or during this exercise.*

1) The trainer introduces the exercise by noting that obligation overload and over-commitment are common sources of stress. She hypothesizes that this group is no exception and asks for a show of hands from participants on the following questions:

✔ How many people have commitments and obligations that require your time and energy on a regular basis (eg, Rotary meetings, practicing Suzuki cello with your child, bowling league, church/ community board, daily exercise, etc)?

☞ *Give some examples of your own and elicit several from the group. These should be regular, on-going, predictable commitments.*

✔ How many people have experienced during the past year some new commitment or obligation that requires your time and energy?

☞ *Again, give examples (eg, fund-raising for charity, a new baby, a sick family member to care for, an exercise program, organizing the staff picnic, different job duties, etc), and invite participants to share a few.*

✔ How many people have ever felt overwhelmed by the number or intensity of their commitments or obligations?

   ☞ *You may want to say, "Whew, I'm glad I'm not the only one!" or "Welcome to the human race!" or "You're in the right class, then!" to those who raise their hands.*

✔ How many people believe that they could reduce some of their current stress by cutting out some obligations?

   ☞ *Usually most people will say yes. If some do not, congratulate them and tell them that their skills will be particularly helpful in the next step, or invite them to stick around and watch everyone else squirm!*

2) The trainer uses the data generated in *Step 1* to amplify her introduction to obligation overload, covering some or all of the following points.

● **Obligations and commitments are promises we make** that bind us to a course of action. These "ought-tos" and "want-tos" of life can be a source of rich joy and reward as we put our beliefs and values into action. They can also be a source of stress when we overload ourselves with too many.

● **Some obligations we honor are just habits or secondhand mindsets** that we hold on to without careful appraisal of their cost, benefit, or meaning (eg, having floors so clean you could eat off them, feeling responsible for others, believing that children's needs come before parents', etc).

● **It's easy to take on obligations and make commitments**—all it requires is a nod of the head. Following through is a lot more demanding. We have a remarkable capacity for selective amnesia. Even when we're already overburdened with "have-tos" and "want-tos", we continue to say that risky four-letter word, "SURE!"

● Many commitments have no designated end point, and often those that do are often just stepping stones to new responsibilities.**Getting out of obligations is a lot harder than getting into them**. Saying "no" or "no more" is much tougher than saying "yes."

● The result?**Obligation overload**. We continue to pile on commitments without unburdening ourselves of previously promised responsibilities. What a set-up for stress!

3) The trainer asks participants to identify *one obligation or commitment* *they would like to eliminate from their life.*

   ☞ *Draw on examples volunteered previously or stop and generate a list to prime the pump (eg, membership in an organization, chauffeuring kids to baseball practice, paperwork on the job, house cleaning routine, making sack lunches, etc). Encourage people to be specific and practical in their choices.*

4) The trainer asks participants to form groups of four for the next .

   ☞ *This process does not work well with fewer than 4 or more than 6 in the groups. If numbers don't come out evenly, create a few groups of 5.*

5) After everyone is settled, the trainer reflects that giving up obligations is difficult because there are a host of internal and external voices that pressure us *not* to change. She invites participants to explore the dynamic of standing up to such pressures in a role-play situation and gives instructions for the first step.

   ➤ Decide among yourselves who will be **Monday, Tuesday, Wednesday, Thursday** and **Friday** (if there are 5-person groups).

   ➤ **Wednesdays** will begin first by explaining what obligation you have decided to eliminate. Be sure to give some details about the situation and the people involved.

      ➤ What meaning does it have for you?

      ➤ Why did you take it on in the first place?

   ➤ Take about 2 minutes to describe in detail the obligation you want to unload.

   ➤ The job of others in the group is to get a vivid picture of *Wednesday's* situation and the obligation he wants to give up. Listen closely and feel free to ask clarifying questions.

6) The trainer interrupts after 2 minutes and gives instructions for "putting on the pressure."

   ➤ Now that *Wednesday* has described the commitment he wants to eliminate, the *other group members* should come up with as many reasons as possible why *Wednesday* should *not* give up this obligation, but should rather continue on with the commitment.

      ➤ Take turns challenging **Wednesday**, doing your best to make him feel guilty, irresponsible and selfish for wanting to give it up.

©1994 Whole Person Press 210 W Michigan Duluth MN 55802   (800) 247-6789

➤ *Do not indulge in character assassination!* Your role is to verbalize the pressures *Wednesday* might feel—both internally and externally—if he really does try to eliminate this obligation.

➤ Meanwhile, *Wednesday* should try to hold firm on his resolve, verbally standing up to each challenge.

➤ If *Wednesday* bogs down under the pressure or needs some help combating specific challenges, someone in the group can offer support, whispering possible responses in *Wednesday*'s ear. Don't let *Wednesday* collapse or renege! Get in there and help!

➤ If the group runs out of ideas for putting on the pressure, repeat some of your arguments so *Wednesday* can practice persistence.

▶ You will have about 3 minutes for each person to practice standing up to pressure. I'll interrupt with a one-minute warning so that *Wednesdays* will have an opportunity for getting in the last word.

▶ Remember, the idea here is to verbalize the pressure, not attack the person. Be firm, but kind!

☞ *Circulate around to observe how groups are handling the process. You may need to restrain a heavy-handed group or encourage reluctant participants to put on more pressure.*

The dialogue process of letting go and being pressured may help some people recognize that they really do not want to give up this obligation. Fantastic! This is a values clarifying exercise. Affirm the clarity and encourage the participant to choose a different obligation to unload.

7) After about 3 minutes the trainer interrupts and announces the next candidate for obligation unburdening. The trainer reviews the instructions and repeats *Steps 5* and *6* until all participants have taken a turn at role playing.

☞ *Mix up the order of the "days" so people aren't anticipating their turn.*

8) When everyone has had a turn, the trainer reconvenes the large group and solicits reactions to the experience. If the following points do not arise spontaneously in the discussion, the trainer may include them as part of a closing.

● There are many good reasons why we should continue with some commitments. It's impossible, however, to continue every commitment forever. Coping with obligation overload is a matter of setting priorities and eliminating activities even though they are meaningful. A meaningful commitment that exhausts us rather than energizes us ceases to be beneficial.

- Some of our reasons for continuing our obligations sound pretty silly when spoken out loud.

- Once we decide to say "NO" to an obligation, our own mind goes to work pressuring us in the same way the groups here did. Our noisy self-messages make it tough for us to follow through on decisions to abandon commitments. It takes persistence and courage to act on our resolve.

- The expectations of others play a major part in keeping us involved when we want "out." In order to take charge of our lives we must overcome the pressure others put on us. Pleasing others at the expense of our own peace of mind is costly to our well-being.

- We *can* say "no" if we practice!—And guess what? The world doesn't end!

TRAINER'S NOTES

Submitted by Pat Miller.

123 METAPHORS 2

In this imagination-stretching process, participants uncover new approaches to a stressful situation.

GOALS

To promote creative approaches to stress management.

To view a current stressful situation from a new perspective that suggests alternatives for coping.

GROUP SIZE

Unlimited

TIME FRAME

20–30 minutes

MATERIALS

Metaphors 2 worksheets for all participants.

PROCESS

☞ *This exercise is not for the novice trainer. You need to be able to "read" the group and play with the pacing to make the process work.*

1) The trainer introduces the exercise by commenting on the need for creative approaches to stress management.

   • **Logic is only one tool we have for understanding our stress** and developing strategies for coping with it. In fact, some research suggests that direct approaches to managing stress are not always the most effective.

   • **Creativity is our natural ally in managing stress**—especially when we are stuck and have trouble seeing options.

   • Metaphors can be a surprisingly powerful way to help us take a new look at our stress and discover new perspectives.

2) The trainer asks participants to choose a stressful situation they are currently dealing with.

   ☞ *Give some examples (eg, "This stress could be as significant as a divorce or as seemingly trivial as a co-worker who hums under his breath or a child who keeps losing her mittens"). Any events that cause distress or any ways that individuals feel "stuck" are appropriate choices.*

While people are reflecting, the trainer distributes **Metaphors** worksheets to participants.

3) After a few moments, the trainer asks if everyone has a specific stress in mind and gives instructions for the first step in the metaphor process.

➤ Describe your stress in 25 words or less in the *top box* of the worksheet.

4) The trainer invites participants to brainstorm some possible metaphors for managing stress (eg, managing stress is like conducting a symphony or fixing a gourmet dinner). As each metaphor is suggested, he records it on newsprint for use in *Step 5* and asks the group to generate a few ideas about how managing stress resembles that metaphor.

☞ *Since this is a force-fit creativity exercise, almost any metaphor will work. If the group has trouble coming up with metaphors, give several examples so that participants have at least 5 or 6 to choose from. Be sure to include metaphors that might be particularly appealing to your audience:*

   + *running an obstacle course*
   + *balancing your checkbook*
   + *managing a political campaign*
   + *operating a gas station*
   + *scaling a cliff*
   + *building a treehouse*
   + *writing a novel*
   + *making a quilt*
   + *planning a party*
   + *naming your first child*

5) After several possible metaphors are listed, the trainer directs participants to apply one of the metaphors to their stressful situation.

➤ Choose a metaphor that appeals to you and write it *in the middle section* of your worksheet, *Managing this situation is like . . . (your metaphor).*

➤ Now consider how that metaphor might apply to the stressful situation. How could managing this situation be similar to your chosen metaphor?

   ☞ *Be sure to give some concrete examples using one of the metaphors and your own stressful situation. Or as a demonstration, you could ask the group to consult with you on your stressor and metaphor.*

➤ Record whatever associations occur to you in the middle section of the worksheet.

6) Participants pair up with someone who has chosen a metaphor that is **different** from theirs. Once everyone has a partner, the trainer gives instructions for sharing.

➤ Whoever has the next birthday starts first.

➤ There are three parts to your sharing.
   ➣ First, take two minutes to describe to your partner the stressful situation and coping metaphor that you chose.
   ➣ Then share the stress management ideas suggested to you by the metaphor.
   ➣ Finally, invite your partner to brainstorm with you about specific ideas for managing your stress more effectively that are stimulated by the metaphor. Write down all the suggestions in the *bottom third* of your worksheet.

➤ I will interrupt you after about five minutes so that your partner will get an equal chance for sharing and consultation.

   ☞ *You may want to interrupt after 2 minutes to indicate time to move on to the brainstorming.*

7) After about 7 minutes, the trainer interrupts and directs participants to switch roles. To help people keep on track, she reviews the three-step process and then announces the 2-minute mark again to make the transition to brainstorming.

8) When the second partner has completed the consultation process (about 7 minutes), the trainer reconvenes the entire group and solicits examples of insights and creative coping strategies that were generated by the process.

9) In closing, the trainer reminds participants that the creative process is a powerful ally in managing stress.

METAPHORS 2

STRESSFUL SITUATION

METAPHOR:
Managing this situation is like _____
in the following ways:

Ideas for more effective stress management suggested by this metaphor:

1)

2)

3)

4)

5)

6)

7)

8)

124 911 EMERGENCY PLAN

In this exploration of coping in crisis situations, participants develop a personalized strategy for emergency stress management. This technique is especially helpful for people who want to change stressful habits such as smoking, alcohol or drug use, overwork, anger outbursts, etc, and for stressful interpersonal relationships.

GOALS

To explore options for coping in acute stressful situations.

To develop a personal strategy for managing stress in a crisis.

GROUP SIZE

Unlimited. Works well with individuals.

TIME FRAME

20–30 minutes

MATERIALS

Blank 3"x5" notecards for all participants; blackboard or newsprint easel.

PROCESS

1) The trainer introduces the exercise with a few comments on managing stress in a crisis:

  ● Stress comes in all kinds of packages—from the long-term strain of unemployment or the breakup of a relationship to the more acute stress of taking an exam or dealing with a belligerent toddler.

  ● The coping techniques that work well for long-term stress are not necessarily effective in emergency situations when we feel over-whelmed, out of control, or on the verge of panic.

2) The trainer asks participants for examples of "crisis" situations where a "panic plan" for managing stress might be useful. All suggestions are recorded on the blackboard or newsprint.

  ☞ *The trainer may need to help participants stretch their concept of emergency situations to include situations such as impulse shopping, bingeing, alcohol or drug abuse, temper tantrums, etc.*

---

3) After a lengthy list has been generated, the trainer asks people to switch gears and reflect on the techniques that have worked for them in coping with emergency situations like these. The trainer records all methods.

☞ *As participants offer ideas, you may want to group them according to the three parts of the **Panic Plan** outlined below.*

4) The trainer congratulates the group on the variety of coping options they have generated and notes that it is helpful to plan in advance how we might handle a crisis.

- In the midst of a crisis we are often in such a state of anxiety, shock or disorientation that clear thinking and creative problem solving are difficult.

- When we feel out of control or on the edge of panic, we need a clear, simple, familiar coping routine to provide some order, direction and sense of power.

5) The trainer introduces the three-step *Panic Plan* for handling any stress emergency.

- Take a **TIME OUT**. First, stop, close your eyes, and take a deep breath. Take several more deep breaths as you go inside yourself and imagine letting go of the tension generated by your stress response in key body areas—head, belly, chest, back, legs, etc.

  After the first wave has passed, try to stay cool and centered for ten minutes before you take any other action. Set a timer if possible so you can really let go and relax. If you can survive ten minutes, chances are good that the crisis will have passed.

- Find an **OUTLET**. Pick up the telephone or a pencil and verbalize your feelings and needs. Talk to a trusted friend. Write down what provoked your stress in a journal—or on a paper napkin. Get it out of your system so you can leave it behind and get on with your life.

- **GET OUT**. Disconnect from the source of your stress by leaving the situation that provoked it. Don't hang around waiting for the situation to trigger more stress. Get moving. Walk away. Do something else. In most cases you can come back to the issue later with a new outlook and renewed potency.

6) The trainer challenges the participants to create a personal *911 Emergency Plan* for coping with acute stress in the future. She distributes 3"x5" cards to all and instructs the group how to use them.

➤ On one side of the card list several types of situations that typically provoke an acute stress reaction for you.

➤ On the flip side, divide the card into three sections and label them with the three emergency responses: *TIME OUT, OUTLET* and *GET OUT.*

➤ In each section jot down several ideas you could use to manage stress in an emergency. Most of these strategies should be quick and familiar so that they will be easy to implement. But also include one or two new or unusual techniques you may have learned from others here. Check the list we generated for intriguing options.

7) The trainer solicits examples of panic plans from the group and encourages participants to put the card in their wallet for quick reference in an emergency.

VARIATION

■ After *Step 6* participants are divided in groups of three to practice their emergency plans in a role-play situation. The trainer assigns one of the situations generated in *Step 3* to each group. Each person takes a turn practicing their panic plan as other group members act out the scene.

TRAINER'S NOTES

Submitted by Ruth Strom-McCutcheon.

©1994 Whole Person Press 210 W Michigan Duluth MN 55802   (800) 247-6789

125 REST IN PEACE

In this unusual visualization, participants lay to rest negative attitudes, perceptions and patterns that cause them stress.

GOALS

To identify adaptive patterns that have outlived their usefulness.

To practice a technique for letting go of stress.

GROUP SIZE

Unlimited; also works well with individuals.

TIME FRAME

15–20 minutes

MATERIALS

Rest in Peace worksheets (p 72) for all participants; **Rest in Peace** script, (p 70).

PROCESS

1) The trainer introduces the basic principles underlying this exercise.

   ● Most of us carry around leftover thoughts, ideas, beliefs, feelings or attitudes that helped us get through a particular difficult situation. In the short run, hostility, despair, denial, perfectionism, cynicism, insensitivity, etc can be effective stress managers, but in the long run they are stress producers rather than reducers.

   ● Periodically we need to clean house by taking stock of our response repertoire and getting rid of those patterns that may once have been effective but now result in negative consequences.

     For example, anger toward your parents may have once been an essential tool to help you separate from them. However, holding on to this antagonism into adulthood can be stressful—and can interfere with the development of satisfying mutual relationships as adults.

2) The trainer invites participants to unburden themselves from some of their outdated and stressful notions.

➤ We are going to experiment with a visualization process that can be applied whenever you want to let go of unwanted stress and/or dysfunctional coping patterns.

➤ Close your eyes, take a deep breath or two, and relax.

3) The trainer slowly reads the **Rest in Peace** script, pausing as appropriate to promote vivid visualization.

4) As soon as most participants have returned their awareness to the here and now, the trainer distributes **Rest in Peace** worksheets to all, and instructs participants to write down on the grave marker those stressful attitudes, feelings and patterns that they decided to bury.

5) After 2–3 minutes the trainer directs everyone to find a partner and spend about 5 minutes together sharing their experiences with the visualization and the content of their worksheets. He may pose the following questions to facilitate discussion:

➤ What images came to your mind during the visualization?

➤ What negative patterns did you want to bury? How do you imagine this will change your life?

➤ How did you feel about letting go?

6) The trainer reconvenes the entire group and solicits reactions to the experience and potential applications.

VARIATION

■ Close the exercise with a "cremation service" where participants burn their worksheets or post all worksheets in a group "graveyard."

TRAINER'S NOTES

Submitted by Richard Boyum.

REST IN PEACE Script

Take a moment now to tune in to yourself and tune out
whatever may be distracting . . .
Take a deep breath . . . and let it out with a soft sigh . . .

Focus on your easy breathing that quiets and calms you . . .
Take another deep breath . . . and as you breathe out . . .
let go of whatever is cluttering your mind . . .

As you continue to breathe freely and easily . . .
allow yourself to become aware of some of the negative attitudes . . .
perceptions . . . feelings . . . patterns . . .
that may be causing you unwanted stress . . .

Even though these patterns were once essential or effective in managing
your life . . . you need to let go of them now . . .
lay them to rest . . . so that you can have peace . . .

Let this procession of negative thoughts, feelings, attitudes
pass before your mind's eye . . .
Try to give each image a name or symbol so that you can bring it into
sharper focus . . .

> ☞ *Allow some time here for people to get in touch*
> *with these negative stressors and visualize them.*

Now imagine yourself in a funeral parlor . . .
In a room with a special container . . .
that can be closed and sealed for burial . . .
Notice that the container is open now . . .
ready to receive any negative thoughts . . .
any attitudes or feelings that are distressing to you . . .
All of those unhealthy patterns you would like to give up . . .

Now imagine holding all these unwanted thoughts and beliefs
in your hands . . .
Then one-by-one place them in the container
so you never have to see them again . . .

As you are putting your unwanted relics in the container
and preparing to close the cover . . .
consider who you would like to join you in this special place . . .
to witness this surrender . . .

Imagine that these friends are now standing with you . . .
supporting you . . . remembering with you . . .
mourning with you the passing of these comfortable old habits . . .

> ☞ *Pause here long enough for participants*
> *to image the arrival of their supporting cast.*

Now it's time to close the cover of the container . . .
and journey to the cemetery where a special place
has been prepared to accept your container . . .
This could be a crypt, or a grave or a monument . . .
whatever seems right to hold your burdens . . .
Invite the others to join you as you take your container
to its final resting place . . .

Once you and the others reach the cemetery . . .
place your container into the grave and cover it . . .
or close the door of the crypt . . .

Allow yourself to experience all of your feelings . . .
as you say "goodbye" to these parts of you . . .
as you feel the support of those around you . . .

Imagine now a marker being placed on the grave . . .
A marker that commemorates each of the things
that you are putting to rest . . .

> ☞ *Pause here for this image to form.*

Now imagine yourself and your companions
slowly withdrawing from the grave site . . .

Know that at any time you choose . . .
you can return to this site in your imagination . . .
and ponder what is buried here that you no longer need . . .

Take a moment to complete your journey back to this place . . .
no longer bearing the burdens you have put to rest . . .
Enjoy the peace and calm and freedom
as you return your awareness to this place and the people around you . . .

Stretch a little . . . take a few deep breaths . . .
and prepare to capture some of your images on paper . . .

REST IN PEACE

_____
Name

_____
Date

Here lies my...

_____

_____

_____

_____

_____

_____

_____

*May these things rest in peace
so that I may live in peace!*

Skill Builders

126 GO FOR THE GOLD

In this skill-building exercise, participants examine their personal goal-setting process and explore the effectiveness of organizing their day-to-day decisions toward specific, targeted goals.

GOALS

To assess participants' current level of personal planning.

To illustrate the benefits of regular goal-setting.

To facilitate the development of positive habits and skills that help individuals be productive and reach personal targets.

GROUP SIZE

Unlimited.

TIME FRAME

30–40 minutes

MATERIALS

Copies of the **Go for the Gold** and **Target Inventory** worksheets for all participants.

PROCESS

1) The trainer distributes **Go for the Gold** to each participant and informs the group that this session is an exercise in personal goal setting.

   As a way of assessing the effectiveness of their current goal-setting practices, participants are asked to complete the worksheet according to the following instructions.

   ☞ *Allow time for participants to complete each step before moving on to the next instruction.*

   ➤ Let your mind wander over what you've been trying to accomplish during the past month (eg, clean out the garage, implement a new accounting system, lose five pounds, finish a project, get along better with your mate, etc).

   ➤ Focus on one goal you set for yourself during the past month that you actually accomplished. Write it down under *Goal 1* on your worksheet. Then write a few comments about the results.

➤ Now focus on one goal you set for yourself this past month that you did not reach. Write it down under *Goal 2* and comment on the results.

➤ Answer the questions at the bottom of your worksheet. *What contributed to your success? What contributed to your failure?* Then jot down any additional comments or observations about your goal-setting style or pattern.

   ☞ *Some participants—perhaps a majority—will have difficulty identifying any significant goals. Encourage those who were "goal-less" this past month to make observations and comments about how life flows from day to day without goals, about their excuses for not setting goals, or about how they imagine that clear goals would help them.*

   Assure those who have difficulty that this exercise is intended to help them identify and target one or more goals for the coming month.

2) After all have completed their worksheets, the trainer presents information on the benefits of day-to-day goal setting, alternating group voting questions with points.

   ☞ *As participants raise their hands in response to questions, encourage them to look around the room to check out the group's response.*

✔ How many of you were able to identify a specific goal that you aimed for and reached last month?

   ☞ *Congratulate this group. Ask for some examples and respond to each offering with "Great! Give yourself a gold medal!"*

✔ How many of you not only didn't get the gold, but had trouble identifying specific goals you had been aiming for? Weren't sure what your goals were?

   ☞ *Reassure this group that this is not unusual, and invite them to tune in now for a special training camp.*

   ● If you can't identify a goal now, it's likely that you didn't know what you were aiming for throughout the month. If you spent a whole month without any targeted goals, how did you make decisions about spending your time and energy? Did you just wander through the day waiting for life to give you an agenda?

   ● Goals help target your activity and focus your choices about what you do and when you do it. Without goals you're likely to wander without direction through each day, reacting to whatever bumps into you.

● Living without goals is like driving a car without a steering wheel—foot on the gas, roaring around aimlessly. If you don't know what you are aiming for, you'll surely never know whether you ever get there!

✔ How many of you during the past month felt like you had too much to do and too little time to do it in? And felt stressed as a result? Or felt like you accomplished less than you wanted to?

● Life always presents us with more options than we can pursue, and often leaves us feeling way too busy. That's the major reason for goal setting.

● Without taking stock of what you're trying to accomplish, you'll regularly feel frustrated, pushed and pulled by the possibilities of life, stressed, feeling like you're not getting anywhere.

● Once you target clear goals, and make choices for moving toward them, you can also more easily let go of other possibilities, or at least relegate them to the back burner.

✔ How many of you regularly write down your goals?

● Writing your goals, or even listing your short-term tasks can reduce your stress.

● First, you'll be clear about your targets and should be able to remember them.

● Second, putting your goals in writing increases your commitment to them and enhances the likelihood that you'll follow through on your intentions.

● Third, written goals help you resist sidetracks and diversions that may regularly tempt you.

✔ How many of you would like to be more productive next month than you were last month? How many think that you can be?

● Everyone can be more productive—intentional goal-setting is the key. Remember, you can be *busy* without being productive. And you can be productive without reaching the personal targets that are important to you. If you get your priorities clear, set specific goals and write them down, you can reach more targets that are important to you.

✔ How many of you aren't even sure what you really want for yourself?

● It is important to identify what you want to improve or change, but sometimes that's not so easy to discover. The next step in this exercise will help you start focusing on some potential goal areas in your life.

3) The trainer distributes a copy of the **Target Inventory** worksheet to each participant and gives instructions for the goal-setting process.

➤ Part 1 of this worksheet lists 10 areas of life that affect your well-being. Consider these areas one-by-one and determine how satisfied you are with that area of your life right now.

➤ Rank your level of satisfaction using the 0–5 scale in the middle column (0 = totally dissatisfied, 5 = totally satisfied).

☞ *Allow 1–2 minutes for this process. If anyone has difficulty with the scale, remind them that the point here is to isolate potential areas for attention.*

➤ Now go back and consider each life dimension again. This time think about what would make this area of your life more satisfying. In each section of the right-hand column write one response to fit the phrase, *"I would be more satisfied with this area of my life if . . ."*

➤ Don't worry too much about being practical, just jot down one of your "wishes" for improving this part of your life.

4) After everyone has taken a broad look at their life satisfactions, the trainer helps people focus on isolating a specific goal for the next month and determine whether or not they intend to pursue it. Participants complete *Part 2* of the **Target Inventory** worksheet, following the trainer's instructions.

➤ Look over your **Target Inventory** and choose one area where you would like to experience more satisfaction in the next month. Write your choice in *Part 2* of your worksheet.

➤ Next, list all the ways you can imagine that would make this part of your life more satisfying.

☞ *Give a few examples in two or more life areas here (eg, I'd be more satisfied with my job if I had a better space to work in, if there weren't so much noise, if there were more opportunities for informal socialization, if I could complete projects all the way to the end without getting interrupted, if my supervisor were more supportive, etc). Use your imagination to help people stretch their wishing muscles.*

Allow plenty of time for people to generate these lists.

➤ You have just completed the first step in effective goal-setting: pin-pointing specific troublesome aspects of your life that you may want to change. The next step involves transforming each of these complaints into a definite goal statement. In *Section C,* convert each of your *"I would be more satisfied . . ."* wishes into a clear goal statement.

☞ *Again, give several concrete examples that correspond to your previous illustrations (eg, improve working space, reduce noise at work, find ways to make positive contact with work associates, reduce interruptions, ask for more support from supervisor or seek it elsewhere, etc).*

➤ Now choose one of these goal statements that you would like to accomplish during the next month. Write it down in *Section C.* Then answer the remaining questions about how you might reach your goal. Once your plan is down on paper, decide whether or not you really want to pursue this goal, and then sign your name.

5) After everyone has finished their goal-setting (5 min) the trainer offers the following final tips for increasing the effectiveness of goal-setting behavior.

● **Make it routine**. Each day pursue your goal at the same time, in the same place, with the same people, etc. Regular patterns help you build positive habits. Also, set regular times for reviewing and updating your goals.

● **Keep your eyes on your target**. Be aware of what you are trying to accomplish. Mull it over in your mind. Focus on it. Organize yourself and your day by making your target a priority. Keep track of your progress—you'll be less likely to be diverted for extended side trips along the way.

● **Be flexible**. Unexpected demands should be expected! So plan them into your day. Remember, your plan is not a straitjacket, it's a tool! So be flexible when you need to, without giving up on your goal.

● **Plan and re-plan**. Out of the muddle of your life, goal-setting can help you determine what it is you want to aim for. It's a skill. Use it regularly. When you feel too busy and scattered to plan—that's the sure sign you need to center in and refocus yourself on clear personal targets.

VARIATIONS

■ If you want to increase participant involvement and interaction, ask people to pair up and share their **Go for the Gold** responses as part of *Step 1*.

■ After *Step 4* allow time for participants to share their personal goals with each other in.

*The inspiration for this exercise came from Leon Tec's outstanding book, **Targets: How to Set Goals for Yourself and Reach Them** (New York, New American Library, 1980).*

GO FOR THE GOLD

What contributed to your success?   What contributed to your failure?

Comments on your personal goal setting process

TARGET INVENTORY Part 1

Date:

Life Dimension	How satisfied	If . . .
Health	0 1 2 3 4 5	
Marriage	0 1 2 3 4 5	
Children	0 1 2 3 4 5	
Extended Family	0 1 2 3 4 5	
Job/Career	0 1 2 3 4 5	
Financial	0 1 2 3 4 5	
Housing	0 1 2 3 4 5	
Social Network	0 1 2 3 4 5	
Leisure Activities	0 1 2 3 4 5	
Values/Faith	0 1 2 3 4 5	

TARGET INVENTORY Part 2

A. Choose one area for focus:

B. I would be more satisfied with this area of my life if . . .

   1) *if . . .*
   2) *if . . .*
   3) *if . . .*
   4) *if . . .*
   5) *if . . .*

C. Goal Statements

   1)

   2)

   3)

   4)

   5)

D. By the end of the month I would like to:

IMAGINE IT

   When I reach this goal the end result will be:

DESCRIBE IT

   Specifically I want to:

PLAN IT

   I can get there by doing the following

   First:

   Second:

   Then:

   Next:

   Next:

   Finally:

I commit myself to this target goal for this month: ___yes ___no

                      _____
                                   Signature

127 SHIFTING GEARS

In this lively skill builder, participants learn specific techniques to manage stress once they've recognized situations in which they need to slow down, "rev" up, or loosen up.

GOALS

To recognize body/mind/spirit signals that indicate the need for a change of pace.

To explore changing tempo as a vital stress management skill.

GROUP SIZE

Unlimited.

TIME FRAME

15–30 minutes

MATERIALS

Copies of the **Gear-Shifting Activities** handout for all.

PROCESS

1) The trainer begins by setting the context for this exercise, covering some or all of the following points.

   ● **Stress is not intrinsically bad for us.** Too much stress for too long without discharging some of the accumulated tension can be hazardous to your health. But too little stress can be deadening to your psyche and spirit.

   ● The key to a healthful lifestyle—and to effective stress management—is the ability to pace ourselves so that we minimize the strain of stress and maximize its benefits.

   ● The complexity of our lives often demands that we **shift gears** several times a day—or several times an hour—in response to the kaleidoscope of challenges we face. Sometimes we need to *slow down*, to let up on the gas and shift into a lower gear. Sometimes we need to *gear up*, to rev ourselves up to meet a challenge. At other times we need to *loosen up*, to discharge tension from physical or mental sources. The tricky part is knowing when to do what!

---

2) The trainer announces that during this exercise participants will be exploring situations that require a change of pace and practicing gear-shifting strategies from each of the three styles.

3) The trainer asks participants for examples of situations when changing gears might be an effective stress management strategy.

> ☞ *Generate lots of examples for each gear shift. Prompt with general scenarios (eg, home, work, December, tax time, etc) and solicit specifics from the group.*

✔ Under what circumstances might you need to *slow down* to manage your stress (eg, racing from one task to another, spinning mind, impulsive behaviors, anxiety or worrying, etc)?

✔ In what situations might someone need to *gear up* in order to cope (eg, before a presentation or performance, preparing for holidays, in a boring meeting, the morning after the night before, etc)?

✔ Under what conditions is it important to *loosen up* (eg, when driving in rush hour, sitting in the bleachers, waiting in line)?

4) The trainer distributes blank paper and instructs participants to fold the sheet in half. She then asks people to focus on their recent experience with shifting gears.

➤ Hindsight is 20/20 vision. Please recall a couple of situations during the past week when changing gears was (or would have been) an effective way to manage your stress.

> ➤ Try to remember at least three or four situations and list them down the left side of your paper with a brief description.

> ☞ *If people have difficulty focusing on specifics, ask them to remember their ups and downs today or yesterday. Or extend the time period to a month. Be sure everyone has at least one or two situations in mind before moving on to the next step.*

➤ Take a moment now to consider how you responded to each of those situations.

> ➤ What action or inaction did you take to manage the stress?
> ➤ What did you do to slow yourself down? To gear up? To loosen up?
> ➤ Briefly describe your response to each situation on the right-hand side of the paper.

5) The trainer solicits examples of techniques that participants used to help themselves *slow down.*

☞ *Encourage people to jot down appealing ideas suggested by others that they would consider trying when they need to slow down.*

As suggestions are made, the trainer may request that the person who volunteered the idea demonstrate it and teach it to the group.

6) The trainer leads the group through two or more *slow* down routines from the **Gear Shifting Activities** handout.

7) *Steps 5* and *6* are repeated for *gear up* and *loosen up* techniques.

8) In closing, the trainer distributes **Gear-Shifting Activities** handouts to all participants and encourages them to experiment with them several times a day for the next week to discover which work best for them in different situations.

VARIATIONS

■ The trainer could sprinkle these gear changers throughout a longer presentation. Pay attention to your own timing and pacing. Insert these techniques to change pace when you sense your own or the group's need to shift.

■ Expand this exercise with additional gear shifters from this and other volumes in the stress and wellness handbook series.

TRAINER'S NOTES

Submitted by Mary O'Brien Sippel.

GEAR-SHIFTING ACTIVITIES
SLOW DOWN TECHNIQUES

10-SECOND BREATHING
In an acute situation, when your mind or body is racing out of control, slow down your breathing to a 10-second cycle, 6 breaths a minute. Find a clock or watch with a second hand and inhale for 5 seconds (odd number on clock face) then exhale for 5 seconds (even number). Keep it up for 2–5 minutes, or until your pace slows down.

60-SECOND BREAK
Close your eyes and take a deep breath. Visualize yourself lounging on a sunny beach or watching the sunset or relaxing in the shower or sauna.

5-MINUTE VACATION
Close your eyes and take a few deep breaths. Then visualize a favorite vacation place or activity. Let your imagination carry you away to a special spot that's refreshing and relaxing.

CHEST MASSAGE
Relax your chest muscles and open up your breathing with a vigorous massage along the midline and across the chest below your collarbones.

BOTHER LIST
Write down a list of all the worries, pressures and concerns that are crowding your mind and clamoring for attention. Then burn the list or tuck it in your wallet for later attention.

PEACEFUL FOCUS
Focus on something pleasant and beautiful in your immediate environment (a blade of grass, a painting, a color). Concentrate on the beauty you see and breathe it in. Allow that beauty to slow you down.

GEAR UP TECHNIQUES

STRETCH AND MOVE
Stand up and stretch. Arch your back and stretch your arms and fingers out wide. Hold that posture for awhile and then let go. Now move your body all around to get the blood pumping. Clap your hands. Jump up and down. MOVE!

EXHILARATION BREAK
Imagine yourself somewhere exciting, exhilarating or awe-inspiring (eg, standing on a cliff above the ocean, performing for a large audience, cheering at an exciting football game, crossing the finish line at a race, laughing uproariously with friends, peering over the rim of the

Grand Canyon, giving birth or watching birth). Let the vividness of that vision charge up your batteries.

PEPTALK

Give yourself a peptalk. Use your best persuasive powers to motivate, encourage, cajole, support, cheer, challenge yourself. Ask somebody else to join in!

STIRRING MUSIC

Turn on some lively music like a march or a mazurka. Start moving. Dance. Bounce. March. Sing along. Get involved. Let the music pump you up and pull you along.

BODY BRACER

Gently pat or tap all over your body in an energizing rhythm. Keep it up until you tingle all over and are charged up.

EXERCISE

Vigorous exercise of any kind is a sure-fire way to get geared up. Add a creative twist for some extra punch.

LOOSEN UP TECHNIQUES

PRETZEL

Imagine that your body is all tied up in knots and only you know how to untie them. Beginning with your toes and gradually moving up the body, tense and relax each set of muscles. Visualize that you are tightening the knots as you tense the muscles and picture yourself undoing the knots as you relax the muscles and let go.

BREATHE INTO TENSION

Close your eyes and take a deep breath. As you become aware of any points of tension, "breathe into" that spot, allowing the breath to bring calm to the area and carry away tension as you exhale.

SELF-MASSAGE

Reach across your body and massage the muscles of your neck and shoulder with long, firm strokes. Knead any especially tight areas with firm, circular or back and forth motions. Then repeat the process on the other side. With both hands massage the base of your skull with firm, circular strokes. Continue over the scalp and face, stopping to give special attention wherever you notice tension. Don't forget the jaw!

SHAKE A LEG

Stand up and shake an arm, a leg, the other arm, the other leg, your whole body. Then take a deep breath and let yourself go limp all over.

128 OPEN UP

Participants use a paper bag to explore the potential of self-disclosure as a stress management technique and generate a list of helpful "ears" for coping with tough times.

GOALS

To present the benefits of talking about stress as an effective coping technique.

To practice self-disclosure.

To raise consciousness about resources for help in managing stress.

GROUP SIZE

Unlimited.

TIME FRAME

45–50 minutes

MATERIALS

Paper lunch sacks for all; 2–3 popular magazines for each participant; glue or tape, markers; blackboard or flip chart, list of local community helping resources.

 This exercise requires advance preparation by the trainer. Compile and duplicate an annotated list of community resources participants might want to consult for assistance in managing stress.

*The list should cover **traditional mental health providers** (counseling/mental health centers, public and private social service agencies, hospital outpatient services, chemical dependency treatment programs, church-related services, private practice counselors, psychologists, psychiatrists, etc), other **professional helpers** (eg, clergy, school counselors, etc), **self-help groups** (eg, AA and related 12-step programs, grief and other support groups, etc), and **adult education offerings** (eg, workshops of self-improvement classes in parenting, stress management, time management, etc).*

Asking for help is a difficult proposition for most people. To ease the process as much as possible, be sure the list includes addresses, phone numbers, names of contact persons and information on what to expect (eg, fees, services, times, philosophy/style of treatment, etc).

PROCESS

1) The trainer begins the exercise by asking how many participants talk with other people about the stress in their lives.

   After a show of hands he asks the group to give examples of the types of stress people typically discuss with family, friends and co-workers (eg, child-rearing challenges, minor frustrations at work, time pressures, local politics, poor service from stores or utilities, etc).

2) The trainer asks how many people have held themselves back from talking about a stress they experienced because they felt embarrassed, ashamed or uncertain about how they would be perceived.

   After a show of hands he solicits examples of stressors that are more difficult to share with others (eg, failure at school, sexual difficulties, trouble with the law, alcohol or drug abuse, arguments or violence in the family, approaching death, etc).

3) The trainer presents a chalktalk on the obstacles of talking about stress and the benefits of opening up as a strategy for managing it. He uses the data generated by the group in *Steps 1* and *2* to illustrate the following points.

   - **Confiding in others is a natural impulse following major life upheavals** such as divorce, death or childbirth. We are less likely to talk with others about life stressors that seem embarrassing or shameful.

   - **Our culture values individualism and self-reliance.** Most of us believe that we should be able to manage on our own anything that life deals us. If not, our self-esteem sags. We feel like failures. We're embarrassed to admit our inadequacy. So when we're under stress, we often keep it to ourselves.

   - **Family taboos against self-disclosure can also run deep and stifle our urge to open up to others.** We don't want to seem disloyal. We shudder at the the possibility of appearing self-centered or weak. We fear judgment or criticism. So we clam up.

   - Too bad! **If we withdraw rather than speak up when we're under stress, we cut ourselves off** from emotional support that could nurture us in difficult times. We lose the comfort of discovering that others have experienced similar pain. And we miss the good advice they may have to offer.

● **Confession is good for the body as well as the soul.** Studies have shown that people who do not confide their problems in others suffer more physical symptoms than those people who find a sympathetic listener and share their burdens.

4) The trainer announces that participants will have an opportunity to experiment with self-disclosure as a strategy for managing stress. He distributes a paper bag, 2–3 magazines, a marker, and glue or tape to each participant, then explains the procedure.

➤ Think for a moment about the stress in your life. What types of stressors do you typically share with others? What kinds of stressors are you more likely to keep inside and not share with other people?

➤ Pretend that this bag represents you. The outside of the bag is the picture you present to the world, while the inside is all the things you keep hidden inside.

➤ Now look through the magazines and tear out any pictures, slogans, ads, cartoons, headlines that remind you of the major and minor stress in your life—a crying baby, a hectic office, teenagers, money problems, alcohol or drugs, unstable world conditions, whatever upsets you. Tear out anything that strikes you as symbolic of your stress. Use the markers to personalize the images if you want.

☞ *If participants object to tearing the pictures and ask for scissors, tell them that it's an imperfect world, and they'll have to make do with tearing. Suggest that putting up with imperfections may be one of their stressors.*

5) After about 10 minutes the trainer interrupts and gives instructions for making the bag collage.

➤ Now take the stressors and divide them into two piles—those you talk about in the outside world, and those you keep inside.

➤ Glue or tape the "outside" stressors on the outside of your bag to represent the stress you disclose to others. Put all the rest inside the bag. Close the bag as tightly as you want.

6) The trainer divides the participants into groups of four and gives instructions for discussion.

☞ *Usually, trainers avoid grouping friends together, but it's all right for this exercise. Make the point that even with people we consider friends, self-disclosure is rare. This exercise can help us "break the ice" with people we think we know well. Allow about 4 minutes for each person.*

➤ Each person should take a turn.

➤ Show your bag to the group. Describe a few of the stressors on the *outside* and say something about who you talk to about these pressures.

7) The trainer announces the time every 4 minutes and encourages groups to move on to the next person. After everyone has taken a turn, the trainer interrupts and describes the next step in the process.

➤ Go around the group again, with each person taking a turn.

➤ This time share at least one of your private stressors from *inside* the bag. Talk a little about how it makes you feel and why it causes stress for you.

    ➣ Why have you kept this stressor inside?

    ➣ How does it feel to talk about it in this group?

    ➣ What do you think you need to help you handle it better?

    ☞ *You may want to acknowledge that this is probably a scary assignment for some. Reassure the group, saying something like, "If self-disclosure were easy, we wouldn't need to practice! In this group everyone will share at least one burden. It's easier to confide in someone if they confide in you, too. Use good judgment as you experiment. Take the risk of self-disclosure, but don't share anything you don't want to."*

➤ After you've shared this stressor, decide whether you want to put it back into the bag, or can you put it on the outside? Talk about what would it take for you to be able to put it on the outside?

➤ Each person should take 5 or 6 minutes to open up about one or more of his private stressors.

8) The trainer announces the time at 5-minute intervals to keep the groups on pace. After everyone has taken a turn sharing, the trainer reconvenes the group and makes a few comments on the benefits of self-disclosure as a skill for managing stress.

● Animals withdraw when they're hurt or ill, and many humans do the same when they're under stress. But hiding the problem won't make it go away. Untreated stress is like a thorn in the flesh—it can fester and cause serious problems.

● When we talk through what's bothering, pressuring or upsetting us, we see it from a new perspective. By what we choose to say we often see more clearly the heart of the issue or source of the strain. And we often discover new possibilities for coping in the process.

©1994 Whole Person Press 210 W Michigan Duluth MN 55802   (800) 247-6789

● When you're feeling under stress, talking about it with someone else may make it seem more manageable. Sometimes family and friends are not enough and we need to seek out a special confidante who can help us understand our stress and get some perspective on how to manage it better.

9) The trainer asks participants to brainstorm a list of all the people they might seek out if they wanted to talk about their stress. He records each resource on the blackboard, roughly in categories corresponding to the prepared resources list.

☞ *If people get stuck, suggest some of the following: family or friends, church/community groups, professional counselors, self-help or support groups; social service agencies.*

10) The trainer distributes the prepared list of community resources to participants and asks them to read through it and mark the helping resources they would consider contacting for assistance in the case of stress overload.

TRAINER'S NOTES

129 BIOFEEDBACK

Participants use miniature thermometers to monitor fluctuating stress levels as they practice a simple relaxation routine.

GOALS

To explore the role of self-monitoring (biofeedback) as an essential skill in stress management.

To practice an effective relaxation technique.

GROUP SIZE

Unlimited.

TIME FRAME

20–30 minutes

MATERIALS

Large clock with easy-to-read numerals and a second hand; Biodots or other high-sensitivity skin temperature thermometers for everyone. Biodots are available ($7.50 per 100) from Medical Device Corp, 1555 N Bellefontaine, Indianapolis IN 46202 (317-637-5776).

☞ *If you are located in a cold climate or plan to use the Biodots in winter, ask for some low temperature range dots in case some participants' normal skin temperature is too low to register changes.*

PROCESS

1) The trainer introduces the exercise with a chalktalk on biofeedback.

   • **Biofeedback is the process of tuning in to your body** and learning how to interpret the signals it is sending. Are you thirsty? Hungry? Tired? Tense? Your body will let you know—if you pay attention.

   • **In a perfect world, biofeedback motivates us to action.** We notice our parched lips or dry throat, we search out liquid refreshment. When we notice the rumble that signals hunger, we look for something to eat. When we yawn or notice our energy level plummeting we find a horizontal surface and check out for a nap. When we notice muscle tension creeping up the back of our neck, we stop to stretch and relax.

- **The body is a marvelous self-regulatory mechanism.** It tells us what it needs in very direct and compelling ways. Unfortunately, most of us have lost some of this direct connection to our body signals. We drink to change our mood rather than to satisfy our thirst. We eat by the clock rather than in response to our body's hunger. We override our natural sleep rhythms in order to "party" or to finish some "essential" task. We turn a deaf ear to our tension signals for so long that we don't even recognize when we're uptight.

- Stress management experts use a variety of objective devices to help people get back in touch with their body signals—especially those that typically accompany stress. Once we become aware of any of these body responses through biofeedback, we can learn to change them and reverse the negative effects of stress.

2) The trainer notes that the simplest biofeedback mechanism is a skin thermometer which can alert the wearer to subtle changes in skin temperature which accompany the stress response.

- When we are under stress the blood vessels in our extremities contract so that our blood supply can be redirected to vital organs in the trunk. This is a valuable response if we need to resist or escape a mugging. But when we gear up for stress and then don't take any physical action, tension accumulates and our circulation stagnates in the "ready" mode.

- Research has demonstrated that **people can learn to reverse the stress response** by intentionally relaxing the smooth muscles of the circulatory system, using temperature biofeedback to monitor the changes.

3) The trainer distributes Biodots (or other temperature gauges) to participants. She demonstrates where to place the dot (on the fleshy part of the hand inside the big knuckle at the base of the thumb) and reviews the color spectrum key as outlined by the manufacturer.

  ☞ *Remind people that this is not a competition to find out who is tense and who is relaxed. Each person has a different baseline body temperature. The point here is to monitor* **changes** *in skin temperature that indicate changes in an individual's tension/ relaxation level.*

4) As a warm-up to the relaxation phase of the exercise, the trainer asks participants to assess their current state of tension/relaxation.

©1994 Whole Person Press 210 W Michigan Duluth MN 55802   (800) 247-6789

➤ Close your eyes and take a deep breath. Tune in to your body as a biofeedback instrument. Take another deep breath and pay attention to the level of tension or relaxation you notice in your body right now.

➤ On a scale of one to ten, with 1 representing *extremely tense*, and 10 representing *extremely relaxed*, how relaxed are you right now?

➤ Open your eyes and write that number down somewhere.

➤ Now check out the color of your Biodot and write down the color next to your relaxation number.

5) The trainer invites participants to join in practicing a simple relaxation technique and guides the group through the *I Am Relaxed* routine, using the script on page 96.

6) After 10 minutes the trainer gently interrupts the reverie and asks participants to assess their tension/relaxation level again, using the 1–10 scale and their Biodot color. She then queries the group:

✔ How many people observed a change in the color of your Biodot? What direction? (This is objective biofeedback.)

☞ *You may want to give a low-temp model Biodot to people whose dots did not change color. Encourage them to notice changes in color as the session continues.*

✔ How many people changed in your perception of tension/ relaxation before and after the 10-minute breathing meditation? (This is subjective biofeedback.)

7) The trainer invites reactions from the group and weaves their insights into her motivational comments.

● Don't expect to become an expert overnight. It takes practice both to tune in to your body signals and to relax on demand.

● Practice this 10-minute routine once or twice a day for a few weeks. Soon you will find yourself calling on this technique whenever you want to manage daily tension.

VARIATIONS

■ A sensory biofeedback process such as *Body Mapping* (p 21) or *Body Scanning* (*Wellness 2*, p 113) could be used before *Step 4* to help participants tune in to their body signals of tension.

■ In a multi-session course, give participants several Biodots so that they can wear them around the clock to monitor stress levels and the effectiveness of relaxation or other stress management strategies.

Participants keep a diary and share their insights about specific stressors and relaxation patterns at a subsequent meeting.

■ Headache sufferers may benefit from practicing the **Warm Hands** autogenic routine (**Stress 3**, p 124), using a Biodot for biofeedback.

■ Try Biodots with a variety of brief tension tamers (eg, *Giraffe*, p 113; *60-Second Tension Tamers*, **Wellness 1**; *Take a Deep Breath*, **Wellness 2**; *Stretch*, **Stress 1**, etc) or longer relaxation processes (eg, *Hot Tub*, p 115; *Unwinding*, **Stress 1**; *Wellness Meditation*, **Wellness 4**; *Count-down to Relaxation*, **Wellness 3**, etc).

■ To demonstrate the impact of increased tension on body temperature, experiment with Biodots and stress-provoking experiences (eg, *Obligation Overload*, p 56; *Breath-Less*, **Stress 1**; *Tension Hurts*, **Stress 1**; *Marauders*, **Stress 3**, etc).

TRAINER'S NOTES

I AM RELAXED Script

*Find a comfortable, relaxed posture with your body balanced and arms
   supported . . .   Close your eyes and breathe slowly in and out . . .
   Enjoy the pleasure of feeling yourself breathe . . .*

*As you breathe in . . . mentally hear the words "I AM". . .
   As you breathe out . . . say to yourself, "RELAXED". . .*

*Try that for yourself . . .   Tell yourself "I AM" as you slowly breathe
   in . . . and say "RELAXED" as you slowly exhale . . .*

*Continue to breathe like this for the next 10 minutes . . . focusing on your
   breathing and the words, "I AM . . . RELAXED". . .*

*Count your breaths on your fingers as you go . . .   The best pacing will be
   about 40 breaths in 10 minutes . . .   This is much slower than the
   average pace of 12–18 breaths per minute that we are accustomed
   to . . .   so after 10 breaths you may want to open your eyes . . .
   look at the clock . . .   and see if you can adjust your pace to about 4
   breaths per minute . . .*

*Don't get preoccupied or worried about your timing . . .   Just focus on
   your breathing . . . relax . . . and enjoy the process . . .*

*If you lose track counting . . . just start over again, focusing on breathing
   slowly and saying "I AM . . . RELAXED". . . on each breath. If any
   other thoughts come to your mind . . .   just let these distractions pass
   right through and return your attention to your slow breathing and
   counting . . .*

*Take a deep breath and say "I AM". . . then exhale saying
   "RELAXED". . . and keep that slow, steady rhythm in your
   breathing . . . I'll let you know when it's time to stop . . .*

Planning
& Closure

130 A-B-C-D-E-F-G PLANNER

Participants use a 7-step process to devise a concrete plan for managing one life stressor more effectively.

GOALS

To learn and apply a systematic planning process.

To elicit personal commitment to change.

GROUP SIZE

Unlimited.

TIME FRAME

20–30 minutes

MATERIALS

A-B-C-D-E-F-G Planner worksheets for everyone.

PROCESS

1) The trainer announces that during this segment participants will engage in a step-by-step planning process they can use to draw up a practical plan for coping with stressful life situations, events, habits or attitudes.

2) Participants are invited to reflect on what they have discovered during the learning experience and decide on one stressor they would like to manage more effectively, using some of the approaches explored by the group.

   ☞ *To prime the pump, recall several stressors that have been mentioned in previous discussion (eg, children's bedtime, deadlines at work, IRS audit, illness, divorce, harsh weather, loneliness, meddling relatives, etc) and encourage people to choose one of their own that they are determined to cope with more successfully.*

3) The trainer distributes **A-B-C-D-E-F-G Planner** worksheets and guides participants through the planning process, giving examples as needed and adjusting the pace to the rhythm of the group.

   ➤ First, at the top of the planner, identify the stressor you're going to tackle.

➤ In *Section A*, define the problems you experience in relation to the stressor. For example, if your stressor is *deadlines at work*, you might state the problem: *"My problem is feeling pressured to accomplish tasks in a specific amount of time,"* or *"My problem is unrealistic expectations,"* or *"My problem is poor time management."*

You may want to describe the problem in several ways to get a better perspective on what is really stressful for you.

➤ In *Section B*, you have an opportunity to get clear about what you want. How do you want this situation to be different? What changes would you like to see? What outcome are you hoping for?

➤ Now for the time of reckoning. We all know that attitude is a key ingredient in our perception of stress. Attitude is also instrumental in managing stress.

Stop and check yourself out. What is your attitude about this problem?

➤ How hopeful do you feel? Mark your current feeling on the 1–10 scale in *Section C*.

➤ How committed are you to solving the problem? Mark the intensity of your desire to change on the 1–10 scale.

➤ Now total your two numbers. If the total is less than 10, the plan you develop doesn't have much chance for success. You may want to revise your problem statement and/or consider how you might improve your attitude scores.

➤ In *Section D*, your task is to redefine your problem in terms of a challenge. Try switching from a "complaining" mode that discourages problem-solving to an "exploring" mode that invites creativity.

➤ For example, if your problem statement is *"unrealistic expectations,"* the challenge might be, *"to clarify what is expected by whom—including myself,"* or *"to explore what is realistic and unrealistic."*

➤ Now that the challenge is in focus, it's time for some creativity. What activities could help you meet that challenge?

➤ In *Section E* jot down any ideas that come to mind. Try to come up with at least 8 or 10 ideas for fulfilling the challenge you have posed.

➤ Before moving on, look over your list in *Section E* and make your plan. Which of these actions appeal to you? Which will really help you move toward your goal?

➤ Go back and cross out the *could* and write in **would** for those actions you are willing to undertake.

➤ Once you have some concrete actions in mind, the next step is to devise a strategy for implementing your plan.

➤ *Section F* provides an opportunity for you to solidify your commitment by outlining when, where and for how long you will pursue each of the items in your plan.

➤ Take some time to record the commitment you want to make.

➤ Finally, you need to reward yourself. The biggest reward will be intrinsic changes and their impact on the stressor that has been bothering you, but you might want to plan one or more rewards for yourself (eg, a manicure, a round of golf, a new toy, tickets to a play or concert, or other special treats) along the way.

➤ Choose one or more rewards to build into your plan and write them in *Section G*.

4) After the planning process is completed, the trainer may solicit examples of challenges and plans from the group and remind participants that the ABCDEFG process can be used any time they want to develop a strategy for dealing with specific stressors.

VARIATION

■ As a part of the brainstorming process of *Section E*, participants could pair up with a neighbor or two, take turns reading their challenge statements, and brainstorm possible activities together.

A-B-C-D-E-F-G PLANNER

 A   **What's the problem?**

My problem is . . .

B   **What do you want?**

I want . . .

I want . . .

I want . . .

I want . . .

I want . . .

C   **What's your attitude?**

It's hopeless   I'm hopeful

1	2	3	4	5	6	7	8	9	10

MY ATTITUDE TOWARD THE PROBLEM

No desire   intense desire

1	2	3	4	5	6	7	8	9	10

MY COMMITMENT TO SOLVING THE PROBLEM

D   **What's the challenge here? Redefine your problem as a challenge?**

My challenge is . . .

E **What activities could help you meet that challenge?**

I could . . .

I could . . .

I could . . .

I could . . .

I could . . .

I could . . .

I could . . .

F **How and when will you carry out your plan? How many times By when? For how long?**

G **How will you reward yourself?**

131 SO WHAT?

This quick and easy planner challenges participants to summarize what they have learned and apply it in concrete ways to their life situations.

GOALS

To review key concepts from the learning experience.

To articulate possibilities and plans for implementing stress management principles in daily life.

GROUP SIZE

Unlimited; also works well with individuals.

TIME FRAME

10–15 minutes

MATERIALS

What? So What? Now What? worksheets for everyone.

PROCESS

1) The trainer distributes the **What? So What? Now What?** worksheets to participants and gives instructions for completing the first section: *WHAT?*

   ➤ Think back over this meeting and recall the information and issues we've explored together. Mentally review the key concepts and skills presented.

   ➤ In the top box of your worksheet, labeled *WHAT?* jot down the key concepts and approaches that were covered during this presentation. What was particularly meaningful or significant for you? What intrigued, surprised or bothered you? What do you particularly want to remember?

2) The trainer invites participants to consider possible relationships between what they have learned and their current life stress and lifestyle.

   ➤ Look over your list of insights. Go back and mark those items that could apply to your current life situation, the stress you experience or your coping style.

➤ Now, in the *SO WHAT?* box, write some notes to yourself about how you could apply these insights in your life. What is really relevant to you and your unique situation?

3) When participants have finished writing, the trainer invites them to translate their *SO WHAT?* possibilities into concrete plans for action.

➤ Now that you've recalled what you have learned and considered possible applications in your life, it's time to make some commitment to action.

➤ Use the left-hand column of the *NOW WHAT?* section of the worksheet to identify three situations where you hope to apply what you've learned (eg, during exam week, in discussions with spouse, when I feel overloaded at work, etc).

➤ Once you've picked a few target situations, use the right-hand column to describe exactly how you plan to apply what you've learned in each situation and what changes you hope to see.

4) In closing, the trainer may invite participants to describe one situation and application from their *NOW WHAT?* plan.

VARIATIONS

■ As part of *Step 4* participants could share their *WHATS?* and *NOW WHATS?* in small groups.

■ This simple process is a superb tool for conflict resolution and problem solving as well as a perfect instrument for wrapping up or focusing any discussion. Just ask the sequence of questions:

✔ *WHAT?* What is the problem/issue/point?

✔ *SO WHAT?* What are the deeper issues? The implications below the surface? Why is this important?

✔ *NOW WHAT?* How does this apply to our goals, our plan, our situation? Can we make progress?

Submitted by Lyn Clark Pegg who learned the process years ago from Dr George Pilkey, Director of Counseling at Fulton-Montgomery Community College in Johnstown NY.

What?

So What?

Now What?

132 GROUP BANNER

In small groups participants use the contents of a grab bag to create graphic tributes to what they have learned.

GOALS

To review and affirm insights from the learning experience.

To build camaraderie and group spirit.

To provide a playful and creative counterpoint to more serious subject matter.

GROUP SIZE

Unlimited; works well with small teams in an intact staff setting.

TIME FRAME

15–25 minutes

MATERIALS

Plenty of space for small groups to work on projects.

One banner kit for each small group: large sack containing several sheets of tissue paper in at least four different colors, a strip of newsprint or white shelf paper 6–8 feet long, assorted markers or crayons, two or three old magazines.

Appropriate prizes for winning groups (eg, funny stickers, buttons, certificates, etc).

PROCESS

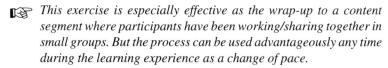 *This exercise is especially effective as the wrap-up to a content segment where participants have been working/sharing together in small groups. But the process can be used advantageously any time during the learning experience as a change of pace.*

1) The trainer instructs participants to rejoin their small group (or team up with three or four neighbors) to collaborate on a construction project.

2) He distributes a paper sack ***Banner Kit*** to each group and announces the guidelines to be followed.

➤ Don't open the bag until I give the word. Inside you will find a variety of items that could be used to make a banner celebrating what you have learned (so far) in this course/session/workshop.

Use all the materials in some way to express your insights.

➤ This is a group project. Everyone should participate in all aspects of the construction—planning, design and execution.

➤ You will have 10 minutes to make your group insight banner.

☞ *If anyone questions the unstructured nature of this assignment, suggest they start with a key phrase from the session (eg, "stress kills," "one step at a time," etc) or a picture from a magazine that typifies stress or coping options.*

3) After about 10 minutes the trainer calls time and asks each group to display its banner somewhere in the room. Participants are invited to promenade the hall viewing each other's creations before settling down to the next content segment.

VARIATIONS

■ As part of *Step 3* the trainer could reconvene the entire group and ask each group to elaborate on the insights represented by their banner.

■ In *Step 2* the trainer could announce that prizes will be awarded for originality, depth of insights, maximum use of materials, etc.

In *Step 3* the banners are numbered. After promenading, participants vote on their choices for each category. The trainer awards appropriate prizes to the winning groups and booby prizes to the others.

133 PAT ON THE BACK

Participants use the colorful PILEUP card game to affirm stress management skills, in themselves and each other.

GOALS

To review the wide variety of options possible for managing stress.

To affirm positive coping efforts.

To provide closure.

GROUP SIZE

Works best: 1) in a workshop or several-session course where participants have interacted frequently and shared significantly; 2) with a small group (6–8 people); 3) with an intact staff or other situation where people know one another fairly well.

TIME FRAME

20–30 minutes

MATERIALS

Blank paper; one deck of *PILEUP* cards for each small group (available from Whole Person Associates Inc, 210 W Michigan, Duluth MN 55802, 800-247-6789).

 The six suits of green positive copers (outlined on pp 110–111) are the only cards from the PILEUP deck that are used for this exercise. Make sure you have a separate set of these 36 coping cards for each small group.

PROCESS

1) Participants rejoin previous discussion groups or form small groups (3-6 people). The trainer distributes to each group blank paper and a set of green coping cards from the *PILEUP* deck and then gives directions for the feedback process.

   ➤ On the left side of your paper write the names of everyone in your small group, including yourself. Leave room between names for jotting notes.

➤ Deal all the cards face down, making sure that everyone has about the same number.

➤ Look at the coping cards you have been dealt. All of these cards represent skills that could be used effectively for managing stress.

➣ Go through your cards, thinking about the skills and the people in your group. Whenever you come across a skill that seems to fit someone in the group as you know him, jot it down by his name.

➣ The descriptions on the cards are meant to stimulate your thinking, so feel free to make up your own interpretations and examples.

☞ *Reassure people that there are 36 skills in all—and they'll probably be able to find several that fit.*

➤ As soon as everyone in your group is finished with the first hand, pass your cards to the person on your right. Look at your new hand and jot down applicable skills for different group members.

☞ *Encourage people to choose skills that they have seen people in their group use (in the learning experience or another setting) or that the individual has described using.*

➤ Keep passing cards around the circle until you get your original hand back.

2) The trainer circulates around the room to monitor the process and helps groups maintain a similar pace. When everyone is about finished, she interrupts and gives further instructions.

➤ Take a look at the skills you've noted for each person in your group. If there is someone on your list for whom you did not find an appropriate matching card, use your own words to describe one or two positive coping strategies used by that person.

➤ Remember, you should have listed one or more skills under your own name as well!

3) The trainer announces that during the next ten minutes participants will join in a celebration and affirmation of the stress management resources of their small groups. She outlines guidelines for sharing:

➤ Each person should take a turn getting a *pat on the back* from everyone else in the group.

➤ Decide who will be the first recipient.

➤ That person should sit quietly and listen closely as other group members disclose the skills they picked for you and describe how they have seen you use the skill in action.

➤ When you're the recipient, and everyone has given you a pat on the back, give yourself one—tell the skill you picked for yourself and give an example of when and how you used it. Brag a little!

➤ I'll keep time and let you know when to put the next person in the limelight.

4) The trainer guides the timing, allowing 2-3 minutes for each person to receive feedback. In closing, she reconvenes the group and asks for observations, comments and insights.

VARIATIONS

■ This exercise can be used exclusively as a self-affirmation process. After the cards are dealt in *Step 2*, the person to the left of the dealer turns over his top card and tells a specific instance when he used that skill effectively. In his description, he should focus on how the skill was used and what happened as a result of using that coper.

■ The next person to the left turns over her top card and describes how she used that skill sometime for managing stress. Continue to rotate around the group, taking turns recalling coping situations and consequences until all the cards have been used.

■ **Pat on the Back** can be used as a warm-up exercise for a more extended presentation on creative alternatives for managing stress.

*The colorful **PILEUP** cards with instructions for 12 additional games are available for $15.95 from Whole Person Press. Quantity discounts available on decks for use in this exercise. Write or call for a quotation!*

*The **PILEUP** cards were originally developed by Whole Person Associates as part of **The Stress Kit**, ©1982, Aid Association for Lutherans.*

©1994 Whole Person Press 210 W Michigan Duluth MN 55802   (800) 247-6789

PILEUP POSITIVE COPERS*

 DIVERSIONS

GETAWAYS:	Spend time alone. See a movie. Daydream.
HOBBIES:	Write. Paint. Remodel. Create something.
LEARNING:	Take a class. Read. Join a club.
MUSIC:	Play an instrument. Sing. Listen to the stereo.
PLAY:	Play a game. Goof off. Go out with friends.
WORK:	Tackle a new project. Keep busy. Volunteer.

 FAMILY

BALANCING:	Balance time at work and home. Accept the good with the bad.
CONFLICT RESOLUTION:	Look for win/win solutions. Forgive readily.
ESTEEM-BUILDING:	Build good family feelings. Focus on personal strengths.
FLEXIBILITY:	Take on new family roles. Stay open to change.
NETWORKING:	Develop friendships with other families. Make use of community resources.
TOGETHERNESS:	Take time to be together. Build family traditions. Express affection.

 INTERPERSONAL

AFFIRMATION:	Believe in yourself. Trust others Give compliments.
ASSERTIVENESS:	State your needs and wants. Say "no" respectfully.
CONTACT:	Make new friends. Touch. Really listen to others.
EXPRESSION:	Show feelings. Share feelings.
LIMITS:	Accept others' boundaries. Drop some involvements.
LINKING:	Share problems with others. Ask for support from family/friends.

*From the **PILEUP** card game, © 1982 Aid Association for Lutherans. Available from Whole Person Press.*

MORE POSITIVE COPERS

MENTAL

IMAGINATION:	Look for the humor. Anticipate the future.
LIFE PLANNING:	Set clear goals. Plan for the future.
ORGANIZING:	Take charge. Make order Don't let things pile up.
PROBLEM-SOLVING:	Solve it yourself. Seek outside help. Tackle problems head on.
RELABELING:	Change perspectives. Look for good in a bad situation.
TIME MANAGEMENT:	Focus on top priorities. Work smarter, not harder.

PHYSICAL

BIOFEEDBACK:	Listen to your body. Know your physical limitations.
EXERCISE:	Pursue physical fitness. Jog. Swim. Dance. Walk.
NOURISHMENT:	Eat for health. Limit use of alcohol.
RELAXATION:	Tense and relax each muscle. Take a warm bath. Breathe deeply.
SELF-CARE:	Energize your work and play Strive for self-improvement.
STRETCHING:	Take short stretch breaks throughout your day.

SPIRITUAL

COMMITMENT:	Take up a worthy cause. Say "yes." Invest yourself meaningfully.
FAITH:	Find purpose and meaning. Trust God.
PRAYER:	Confess. Ask forgiveness. Pray for others. Give thanks.
SURRENDER:	Let go of problems. Learn to live with the situation.
VALUING:	Set priorities. Be consistent. Spend time and energy wisely.
WORSHIP:	Share beliefs with others. Put faith into action.

134 DEAR ME P.S.

This closing/evaluation tool helps participants reflect on what they have learned and focus on potential applications.

GOALS

To conceptualize, relate and apply learning.

TIME FRAME

10–15 minutes

MATERIALS

Dear Me letters generated earlier in the session.

PROCESS

☞ *Pair this exercise with the **Dear Me** icebreaker, p 12.*

1) The trainer introduces this wrap-up exercise by reviewing briefly the content and process of the session.

2) The trainer asks participants to take out the **Dear Me** letters they wrote earlier. Participants are instructed to write a "P.S." to their letters, responding to the following sentence stems as they are posed by the trainer:

> ☞ *Allow plenty of time for people to respond to each stimulus phrase before moving on to the next. Feel free to drop some or add ideas of your own.*

➤ The highlight of this class for me . . .

➤ One place I need to grow . . .

➤ Something I have used (or will use) from this course . . .

➤ One thing I appreciated about the leader . . .

➤ One thing I appreciated about the other participants . . .

3) When the postscripts are completed, the trainer invites participants to make a closing statement, sharing one reflection and one affirmation with the group.

Submitted by Joel Goodman.

Group Energizers

135 GIRAFFE

In this pleasurable visualization, participants learn a simple stretch routine for relaxing the neck and shoulders.

GOALS

To relieve tension in the muscles of the neck and shoulders.

GROUP SIZE

Unlimited.

TIME FRAME

5 minutes

PROCESS

1) The trainer notes that stress-related tension in the shoulders and neck is a common side effect of desk jobs and a frequent cause of fatigue and headaches.

2) Participants are invited to join in a simple stretch designed to relieve tension in those areas. The trainer reads the **Giraffe** script.

TRAINER'S NOTES

©1994 Whole Person Press 210 W Michigan Duluth MN 55802   (800) 247-6789

GIRAFFE Script

Sit in a relaxed, erect position . . .
Take a deep breath and let it out with a big whoosh . . .
Take another deep breath and let your body relax as much as possible . . .

As you are doing this exercise, pay attention to the stretching
and opening you may feel in your neck . . .

Slowly let your head and trunk roll forward . . .
Bring your head lower and lower . . .
stretching your entire spine from top to bottom . . .

When you reach the lowest point, rest there for a moment . . .
Now slowly bring yourself erect again . . .
vertebra by vertebra . . . as if you are stacking the building blocks
of your body one on top of the other . . .
Keep your chin tucked in until you are almost completely erect . . .

Finally, bring your chin and head up . . .
As you make this final movement . . .
imagine that your head is being pulled up by a string . . .
attached to the top from the sky above you . . .

Feel the long stretch in your neck muscles . . .
and be aware of your head . . .
effortlessly floating free above your neck . . .

Imagine that like a giraffe in the jungle you have
an immensely long and graceful neck . . .
that allows you to stretch above the treetops . . .

Look around up there . . .
and enjoy the pleasant sensations of stretching . . .
and floating . . . for as long as you care to . . .
Then slowly let yourself return to normal proportions . . .

136 HOT TUB

In this unusual relaxation experience participants relax in the soothing warmth of an imaginary hot springs.

GOALS

To provide an *in vivo* relaxation experience.

To demonstrate the power of visualization as a tension-reduction strategy.

GROUP SIZE

Unlimited.

TIME FRAME

8 minutes

MATERIALS

Tape recorder and relaxation music (optional).

☞ *Make sure that distractions are kept to a minimum during this exercise. You may want to dim the lights and play soothing music softly in the background.*

PROCESS

1) The trainer invites participants to indulge in a soothing relaxation break.

  ➤ Take a minute to get prepared for relaxation.
    ➤ Take a deep breath and let your body find a comfortable, supported position.
    ➤ Balance your upper body over your pelvis, put your feet flat on the floor.
    ➤ Let your hands fall naturally in your lap with your arms supported by your thighs.

  ➤ Close your eyes and get ready for an imaginary trip to a relaxing environment.

2) The trainer slowly reads the **Hot Tub** script.

  ☞ *Don't hurry! Visualize the images yourself and enjoy the process as you saunter through the script.*

You may want to comment that some people find this type of relaxation experience physically or emotionally uncomfortable. Suggest that anyone who feels uncomfortable at any time during the visualization should open their eyes, stop the mental imagery process, and substitute their own favorite tension reliever.

HOT TUB Script

As you begin to relax . . .
*   focus for a moment on your breathing . . .*

Take a deep breath . . . and as you exhale . . .
*   let go of any worries or concerns that you've been carrying . . .*

Breathe in again . . .
*   letting your chest and belly expand as you inhale . . .*
*   And then exhale . . . with a sigh . . . as you breathe out . . .*
*   letting go of any tension you may be feeling . . .*

As you continue to breathe . . . deeply . . . and rhythmically . . .
*   feel the air*
*   filling every cell in your body . . .*
*   making you feel lighter and lighter . . .*

Imagine that you are relaxing comfortably . . .
*   in a bubbling hot springs . . .*
*   or in a hot tub or whirlpool . . .*

The steaming water enfolds and surrounds you . . .
*   all the way up to your chin . . .*
*   gently massaging your skin . . .*
*   with millions of tiny bubbles . . .*
*   that caress you, and cleanse you . . .*
*   draining away your tension . . . and troubles . . .*

Enjoy the warmth . . . and comfort . . .
*   and support . . . of the water . . .*
*   ☞ Pause.*

Notice how your skin tingles . . . how your face feels full . . .
*   how the pores all over your body . . .*
*   open up to the healing warmth of the bubbling water . . .*
*   ☞ Pause.*

Listen to the sound of the bubbles . . .
  as they percolate through the water . . .
  and gurgle to the surface . . .

Every part of your body is totally relaxed . . .
  supported by the warm water and the tiny bubbles . . .

Your arms and legs . . . feel heavy . . . and warm . . .
  and relaxed . . . yet buoyant . . .

The warmth of the water . . .
  penetrates every part of your body . . .
  allowing you to unwind . . . and let go . . .

Allow the cleansing warmth of the water . . .
  to drain away any tension or discomfort that you are feeling . . .

Watch that tension evaporate . . .
  as the bubbles rise to the surface . . .
  leaving you totally at peace . . .

Stay and enjoy the warmth and relaxation of the water . . .
  enjoy the feelings of comfort . . . and calm . . .
  for as long as you wish . . .

When you are ready . . .
  return to the routine of your day . . .
  refreshed . . .
  revitalized . . .
  unworried . . .
  taking the peace of this place . . . with you . . .

137 HOW TO SWIM WITH SHARKS

This perceptive parody offers humorous advice for dealing with work place environments where some people seem to "go for blood" at every opportunity.

GOALS

To help participants laugh about the stress of dealing with hostile people in difficult situations.

To illustrate that at times self-defense may be the best—or only strategy.

GROUP SIZE

Unlimited.

TIME FRAME

5 minutes

PROCESS

1) After making an appropriate transition from previous content about interpersonal conflict or on-the-job stress, the trainer announces that he has learned five secrets for surviving with sharks that he is willing to share with the group. The trainer reads the *How to Swim with Sharks* script.

*This reading is adapted from an article by Richard J Johns, Johns Hopkins University, that originally appeared in **Perspectives in Biology and Medicine**, 16, p 525-528.*

HOW TO SWIM WITH SHARKS Reading

Nobody wants to swim with sharks. It is common knowledge that sharks attack at every sign of weakness and go for blood at every opportunity. Therefore, do not swim with sharks! It's not enjoyable.

But sometimes people are caught in jobs (or other situations) where they must swim in shark-infested waters. If this happens to you, the following guidelines may help you survive.

Rule 1: Assume that any unidentified fish is a shark.
You can't tell a shark just by looking. Not all sharks look like sharks. Unless you have seen a particular fish remain docile in the presence of bloodshed on more than one occasion, assume it is a shark.

Rule 2: Do not bleed.
If you are injured, cover up the injury, and do not bleed. Experience shows that bleeding prompts an even more aggressive attack by a blood-thirsty shark. If you cannot control your bleeding, do not attempt to swim with sharks. The peril is too great. Get out of the water fast!

Rule 3: Counter any aggression immediately. *Sharks rarely attack a swimmer without warning. Usually they start with a tentative, exploratory aggressive action. Recognize this initial behavior as a prelude to an attack and strike back immediately with force. Some swimmers believe that an ingratiating attitude will keep the shark docile and dispel the attack. This is an erroneous belief. Those who try this method can usually be identified by their missing limbs.*

Rule 4: If someone else is bleeding, get out of the water.
If a swimmer has been injured and is bleeding, get out of the water promptly. Do not let your curiosity tempt you to hang around and watch. Once blood is shed, sharks will attack anyone in the vicinity including you!

Rule 5: Use anticipatory retaliation.
In the presence of sharks who have not yet shown any sign of aggressive actions, the skilled swimmer will mount a pre-emptive attack, striking the shark sharply on the nose without warning. This makes it clear to the shark that you, too, are dangerous.

Of course, when swimmers act this aggressively, it's hard to tell the difference between them and the sharks!!

If you must swim with sharks, these rules should help you survive. If you lose a limb or two, consider getting out of the water—sharks are dangerous only in their own protected environment!

138 HUMAN KNOTS

In this group imbroglio participants learn firsthand how to unwind when they're tied up in knots.

GOALS

To demonstrate that it takes effort to reverse the accumulation of tension that accompanies stress.

GROUP SIZE

Unlimited; chaotic, but fun in a large group.

TIME FRAME

5–10 minutes

☞ *This is an excellent introduction or wrap-up to a presentation on the physical effects of stress and/or the techniques and benefits of relaxation.*

PROCESS

1) The trainer asks participants to stand up, move to an open area and gather into circles of 8–10 people each.

   ☞ *Don't worry about exact numbers. Any size group from 6 to 20 or more will work, but 8–10 is easy to manage.*

2) Once groups are formed, the trainer explains that this exercise will provide a lively demonstration of a familiar process related to stress management. He then demonstrates the *human knots* process with one group as he describes it to everyone.

   ➤ First, close your circle so you can easily reach across and grasp the hands of two different people who are **not your immediate neighbors.**

      ☞ *The trainer may have to help some groups get properly connected. Make sure no one is hooked up to a neighbor, and everyone is gripping the hands of two different people.*

   ➤ Now, untwist yourselves so that you are back in a single circle. Hands can turn in hands so no one breaks a wrist, but *don't let go.* Don't panic! This is possible, but it will take cooperative effort to accomplish.

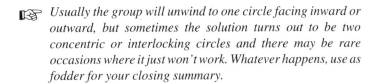 *Usually the group will unwind to one circle facing inward or outward, but sometimes the solution turns out to be two concentric or interlocking circles and there may be rare occasions where it just won't work. Whatever happens, use as fodder for your closing summary.*

3) After all groups have untied themselves, the trainer reassembles everyone and solicits ideas about how this experience relates to stress management. He affirms all suggestions made by participants and adds the points below in summary.

● In times of acute and chronic stress, muscles may actually "tie up in knots" as tension accumulates—often without our conscious awareness.

● It is possible to reverse the process—to untangle the knots, but it takes awareness, effort and cooperation on our part! Simply yanking against the tension only tightens the knot.

TRAINER'S NOTES

Submitted by Glenn Bannerman.

139 MERRY-GO-ROUND

In this rowdy energizer, participants discover the stress of taking on too many burdens.

GOALS

To demonstrate the strain of accumulated stress.

To experience physical and emotional symptoms of stress.

GROUP SIZE

Works best with 8–20 people.

TIME FRAME

5–15 minutes, depending on group size and time allotted for discussion.

MATERIALS NEEDED

Box or bag filled with an interesting variety of (unbreakable) items that can be held in one hand.

☞ *Prepare a group of objects—the zanier the better—beforehand, or collect items on the spot from participants (eg, hat, umbrella, credit card, shoe, keys, notebook, etc) or the surroundings (eg, Styrofoam cup, eraser, paper napkins, etc).*

PROCESS

☞ *This exercise fits well with* ***Obligation Overload***, *p 56.*

1) The trainer announces that participants are about to join in an amusing demonstration of stress pileup.

2) The trainer asks everyone to stand and form one large circle. She gives each person an object to hold and outlines the *Merry-Go-Round* process:

   ➤ We are going to pass these items around the circle from one person to the next, keeping the objects moving at all times.

   ➤ We will pass them as quickly as possible, trying not to drop anything.

   ➤ When something is dropped, the person who dropped it is eliminated, but the object stays in the game. Before he sits down to observe the process, he picks up the dropped item and gives it to the next person along with any others he had been holding.

➤ The people remaining in the circle will start passing all the items again. As soon as something drops, the person with butterfingers sits down after handing her burdens on to the next person.

3) When only a few people are left and the burdens are unmanageable, the trainer thanks participants for the demonstrations, reconvenes the group and asks for insights about the process. The questions below should stimulate discussion.

✔ How did you feel during the various stages of the game? Was it stressful at all? Did you notice any physical sensations? Strong emotions?

✔ How did it feel to be on the receiving end of several objects at once? To get rid of a whole bunch?

✔ Once you were out of the game, what did you notice about your physical tension level? What did you notice about the people who were left?

✔ What parallels do you see between this and the stress in your life?

TRAINER'S NOTES

This energizer was inspired at a youth retreat conducted by Rev Emmajane Finney. Em suggests **Far Out Ideas for Youth Groups** *(Rice & Yaconelli, Grand Rapids MI: Zondervan, 1975) as a rich source for clever energizers.*

140 MICROWAVE

In this invigorating stretch break for large groups, participants join in a familiar grandstand sport.

GOALS

To provide an energizing break for participants.

To stretch and release accumulated tension.

GROUP SIZE

Works best with large groups, but an adventurous trainer could make it fun even for a small group.

TIME FRAME

2 minutes

PROCESS

1) At any point when the trainer wants to change the pace or notices that participants are getting restless, she invites everyone to join in an invigorating stretch.

2) After noting that physical activity is the body's natural method for reducing physical stress and tension, she introduces the wave concept and leads the group through the *Microwave* routine.

   ☞ *To set the context for participants, ask them for an example of a spectator wave that will be familiar to all, or give an example of your own (eg, "Since this isn't the 7th game of the World Series at the Metrodome, we'll have to do without homer hankies and try a* **microwave***").*

   ➤ To warm up, let's try a ***very micro-wave***, just waving your right hand only. Stay seated and show off your hand wave.

   ☞ *In the next waves, the trainer should designate the starting point and may vary it with each step. Try left to right, front to back, around the room, etc.*

   Ham it up a little as you direct the process. Exaggerate to get the group loosened up. Your enthusiasm will be contagious.

   ➤ Now let's try a ***micro-microwave***. For this wave you raise and lower your right hand only in sequence around (or across) the room.

☞ *Again, give some verbal support and encouragement to get people on board.*

➤ All right, you've done so well we can move right on to the ***mini-microwave***. This time, stay seated, but put both hands up and down and quietly say "whoopee!" Don't get carried away, though.

➤ Time for the ***microwave***. This time we'll practice standing up, raising both arms, and shouting "whoopee" with a little more enthusiasm.

➤ Okay, now. This is the real thing. This time we will leap up out of our seats with arms stretched high, cheering at the top of our lungs, and then plop down as relaxed as possible until this ***maxi-microwave*** comes around again.

☞ *Have the group practice the whole sequence once first. Chide them as necessary and encourage them to really get involved the next time. With a large group it's fun to try several rounds.*

TRAINER'S NOTES

This exercise was inspired by the 1988 Winter Olympics Opening Ceremony. Thanks to Heidi Graff for her creative inspiration.

141 THE MUSTARD SEED

This parable poignantly illustrates that loss and death are inescapable partners with life.

GOALS

To illustrate that no one is immune from grief.

To demonstrate that we are not alone, even in deep sorrow.

To suggest that those who grow do so not by avoiding death, but by embracing it.

GROUP SIZE

Unlimited.

TIME FRAME

5 minutes

PROCESS

1) The trainer reads the parable of *The Mustard Seed*, which comes from the Buddhist spiritual teachings.

2) The trainer may offer a personal example of her own to illustrate the Buddha's lesson, or may ask for comments and illustrations from the group.

THE MUSTARD SEED Reading

A young woman had a child.

Her child died, and the woman was overcome by grief.

She did not eat or sleep. She wandered from house to house through the streets of her town, carrying her dead child, and imploring each person she met Help me! Give me something to bring my child back to life!

No one could help her. Some pushed her away. Some turned away from her in pity. Others laughed at her and said she was crazy. Finally, one wise woman told her to go to the top of the mountain to see the Buddha. "The Buddha can help you," she said.

So the woman, still carrying her lifeless child, hurried desperately to the mountain and begged the Buddha for help.

"Give me your child," the Buddha said compassionately. "I can help you, but first you must go back to the town and bring me a mustard seed from a house where no one has died."

The woman hastened back to town, eager to carry out the Buddha's instruction and return quickly with a mustard seed. At the first house a young man responded, "I'd like to help you, but my father has died." At the next house she learned from a grandmother about two recent deaths. A child at the next house shared the anguish of losing her mother.

On and on the woman went, from one house to the next, down one street, then another. Everywhere she went, she received the same answer over and over again: "I'm sorry, but one of my family has died." "I'm sorry, but yes, we too have experienced death here."

Finally, at the end of the day, she returned, exhausted, to the mountain.

"Have you brought me a mustard seed?" the Buddha asked.

"No," said the woman, "and I will not keep seeking. For I have seen that there is not one house where people have not suffered."

"Then why have you returned?" the Buddha inquired.

"Because you can teach me the meaning of this,"said the woman.

And this is what the Buddha told her. "In all the world of people everywhere, this alone is the law for all time: all are mortal. Death takes all. Only those who search through their suffering to understand this truth are truly alive."

©1994 Whole Person Press 210 W Michigan Duluth MN 55802   (800) 247-6789

142 REVITALIZE YOUR EYES

In this ancient self-care break participants practice acupressure techniques for relieving tension and strain in a busy body part.

GOALS

To learn strategies for reducing eyestrain and tension.

To provide a relaxation break.

GROUP SIZE

Unlimited.

TIME FRAME

2–5 minutes each

PROCESS

1) The trainer notes that our eyes are especially vulnerable to stress and introduces the ancient technique of fingertip acupressure.

- Our eyes are natural tension collectors: they are always on the job adjusting to external environments (lighting, airborne irritants, temperature) and taxing activities (reading fine print, video monitors, rapidly changing focus.) We rarely give our eyes a break, except during sleep.

- Acupressure has been used for centuries in the Orient to relax the focusing muscles of the eyes and to increase blood circulation. Many schools and factories provide time twice a day for these simple but effective self-care routines.

- Rubbing around the eye socket affects a number of acupressure points that aid in relaxation.

2) The trainer describes and demonstrates each step of the acupressure self-massage, inviting participants to follow along.

➤ Gently close your eyes and relax as much as possible.

➤ Take a deep breath and allow your mind to clear.

➤ Draw your attention inward and let your eyes relax by visualizing the color "black."

➤ Now use your thumbs or middle fingers to massage the pressure point along the ridge of your eye socket, underneath your eyebrow, at the inner corner of your eye.

➤ You'll recognize the pressure point by a sense of tenderness, or even a slight pulsing.

➤ Use a rocking and rolling massage motion, rubbing toward the nose, then away again.

➤ Massage rhythmically to a count of eight. Rest. Then repeat the 8-count massage 5 or 6 more times.

➤ Don't forget to keep breathing deeply.

➤ The second pressure points to massage are on either side of the bridge of the nose, about where your glasses might rest.

➤ Find the tender/pulse spot and grasp it with your thumb and finger.

➤ Massage by squeezing up and down to the 8-count. Rest. Repeat 5 or 6 more times.

➤ The third set of pressure points are along the lower ridge of the eye socket, below the midpoint of your eye.

➤ Use your middle fingers to massage these points. You can brace your thumbs on your jaw for better leverage.

➤ Rock and roll massage for the 8-count. Rest. Repeat.

➤ Continue to relax as you finish this exercise. And when you are ready, open your eyes and let them continue to relax by gazing out the window or across the room.

3) The trainer closes by recommending that participants experiment with this acupressure technique several times a day to prevent tension and suggests that people try eye massage for headache relief.

*Adapted from **Time Well Spent**, an intriguing stress management and planning calendar for teachers by Larry Tobin available through Whole Person Press.*

143 SIGH OF RELIEF

This quick energizer provides an expressive relaxation break.

GOALS

To release accumulated tension.

To increase participants' repertoire of instant stress relievers.

GROUP SIZE

Unlimited.

TIME FRAME

3–5 minutes

PROCESS

1) The trainer invites participants to join in an amusing experiment with tension relief.

   ➤ Imagine for a moment that you've been under a lot of pressure or have been in a dangerous or frightening situation and suddenly the pressure is off, the danger is over.

   Now would you please give a big *sigh of relief*, a "whew!" that says you're glad this close call or tough time is past.

   ☞ *If the group isn't responsive right away, exaggerate your own and goad them into action (eg, "come on now, you don't sound very relieved—let me hear a big WHEW!"). Try getting two or three big sighs before moving on. Sometimes it helps if people stand up.*

2) The trainer then uses a similar format to lead the group through three more tension-relieving sighs.

   ➤ Let's try a *sigh of disappointment:* OOOOOOOH!

   ➤ How about a *sigh of surprise or delight:* OOOOOOOO!

   ➤ And to finish up, a deep *sigh of satisfaction:* AAAAAAAH!

3) The trainer notes that sighing is a quick and easy antidote to tension.

   ● Sighing is the body's natural way to release tension and get more oxygen.

● Sighing exercises the diaphragm, deepens breathing and relaxes tight jaw and throat muscles.

4) Participants are encouraged to try sighing whenever they notice tension.

TRAINER'S NOTES

144 SNAP, CRACKLE, POP

Participants join forces to get their blood moving in this invigorating stress break.

GOALS

To relieve tension.

To promote interaction and energize the group.

GROUP SIZE

Unlimited.

TIME FRAME

5–10 minutes

PROCESS

1) The trainer announces that it is time for an unusual relaxation break and describes the rationale.

   ● Whenever the body is under stress (like sitting in one position for too long), blood flow to the extremities is restricted. Oxygen supply to muscles of the arms and legs diminishes, and wastes build up in the tissues. Tension, fatigue and discomfort often follow.

   ● Getting the blood flow moving again is a quick way to reduce the tension and reverse the stress response.

2) The trainer leads participants in the *do-it-yourself slapdown*.

   ➤ Stretch out one of your arms in front of you. With the other hand, slap down your arm from shoulder to finger tips and back up again.
      ➤ Slap vigorously and rhythmically—but not so hard as to hurt yourself.
      ➤ Try to cover the front and back as well as the top of your arm.

   ➤ Repeat the same process with your other arm and opposite hand.

   ➤ Now use both hands to slap up and down each leg, stimulating the muscles with vigorous, rhythmic claps.

3) The trainer asks for feedback from the group on what physical sensations they experienced and what emotions they felt before, during and after the *slapdown*.

©1994 Whole Person Press 210 W Michigan Duluth MN 55802   (800) 247-6789

4) Participants are invited to experiment with another version of the *slapdown*, following along as the trainer gives instructions.

➤ Please stand up and get together with two of your neighbors. Threesomes should spread out around the room so you have some space to move freely.

☞ *If the group doesn't split evenly in 3's, a group of 4 or 2 will work with some adjustment in the process.*

➤ Decide which of the three will be **Snap, Crackle** and **Pop**.

➤ Okay, all the **Pops** please raise your hands. You get to go first.

> Stand with your knees straight, arms at your sides.

> Now flop over at the waist and let your arms hang loosely down. Try to find an easy, balanced posture.

➤ The **Snaps** and **Crackles** should stand on either side of the *Pops*.

> Your job will be to gently and rhythmically pat down *Pops'* back, starting at the shoulders and proceeding down to the hips.

> Try to stay together and keep up an even tempo in your gentle pats. *Pops* should speak up if the pats are too hard or in an area that causes discomfort.

☞ *Give a starting signal. After about 45 seconds, direct the Crackles and Snaps to gradually slow down the tempo and intensity of their pats until their hands are resting ever-so-lightly on Pop's back.*

5) The trainer leads the trios through two more *slapdown* rounds, giving the **Crackles** and **Snaps** an opportunity to receive a one-minute massage.

6) After everyone has had a turn, the trainer reconvenes the group and solicits reactions from participants.

Submitted by Krysta Eryn Kavenaugh.

©1994 Whole Person Press 210 W Michigan Duluth MN 55802   (800) 247-6789

TRAINER'S NOTES

Resources

GUIDE TO THE RESOURCES SECTION

This resources section is intended to provide assistance for planning and preparation as you develop and expand your stress management training and consulting in various settings.

TIPS FOR TRAINERS P. 136

Time-tested techniques and suggestions for designing presentations and workshops using the exercises in **Structured Exercises in Stress Management Volume 4** to best advantage.

EDITORS' CHOICE p. 137

Recommendations from the editors on their favorite (FOUR****STAR) exercises from **Stress 4** and teaching designs from this volume that tackle the issue of job-related stress.

> Four****Star Exercises: The Best of **Stress 4** p. 137
> Especially for the Workplace p. 139

WINNING COMBINATIONS p. 140

Potential workshop designs using exercises from this volume. Plus notes on natural companion processes from other **Structured Exercises** volumes.

> Job Stress Presentation (60 min)
> Focus on the Physical: Stress and Relaxation (90 min)
> Good Grief Workshop! ($1^1/_2$–$2^1/_2$ hours)

ANNOTATED INDEXES to Stress 4 p. 142

Guides to specific content segments and group activities incorporated in exercises from **Stress 4**, identified by page reference, time frame, brief description and comments on use.

> Index to CHALKTALKS p. 142
> Index to DEMONSTRATIONS p. 144
> Index to PHYSICAL ENERGIZERS p. 145
> Index to MENTAL ENERGIZERS p. 146
> Index to RELAXATION ROUTINES p. 147

CONTRIBUTORS/EDITORS p. 148

Data on trainers who have shared their best process ideas in this volume. All are highly skilled educators and most provide in-house training, consultation, or workshops that may be valuable to you in planning comprehensive stress management programs. Many contributors are also established authors of well-respected materials on stress, wellness, and training issues.

WHOLE PERSON PUBLICATIONS p. 153

Descriptions of trainer-tested audio, video and print resources available from the stress and wellness specialists.

TIPS FOR TRAINERS

Designing Presentations and Workshops Using Structured Exercises in Stress Management Volume 4

Exercise 131, **So What?**, could be used as a model for planning any presentation or workshop.

- **WHAT** do you want people to learn? WHAT do they need/want? WHAT special focus will be important as you tailor your presentation to the group? WHAT information is essential? WHAT resources are available to you and to your participants?

- **SO WHAT?** This is the relevance question. How can you make the concepts come alive for participants and help people apply this information to their own situation? Start with yourself. What does this idea mean to you? How have you struggled with this issue? What strategies have you used in similar situations. What does the research say? Develop many personal examples for the content and concepts you are presenting.

- **NOW WHAT?** Information and reflection are key steps in the learning process, but the bottom line is action. As you plan, be sure to incorporate processes that will engage people in making plans for change. Include periodic exercises that ask questions like: What are the next steps that I need to take? What do I still need to learn?

Why not make a copy of the **So What?** worksheet on page 104 and use it when planning your next presentation?

This volume contains only a few full-session outlines (45–90 minutes). However, several of the short exercises (5–40 minutes) combine well for longer presentations and workshops.

Build a workshop around Exercise 120, **Lifetrap 4: Good Grief**, as described in the outline below. Or use **On the Job Stress Grid** (Exercise 117) as the centerpiece of a work stress presentation.

EDITORS' CHOICE

We chose the 36 exercises in this volume because of their content, diversity and creative approach to some aspect of stress management. We like every single one, and use them all from time to time in our teaching. But we must admit, some are special favorites and others are more applicable in one situation or another. To help you get started, we have nominated our FOUR****STAR specials.

Four****Star Exercises	Page	Comments (Timing)
111 Quips and Quotes	p. 5	A delightful collection of stress-related aphorisms for introductions or for a creative change of pace during a longer workshop. (20–30 min)
113 Dear Me	p. 12–13	Companion exercises; ideal for framing
134 Dear Me P.S.	p. 112	a longer learning experience (half-day or several session). (10–15 min)
119 Stress Sketch	p. 37–40	If you have time, this "projective" stress assessment really helps people tap into their unconscious to visualize their patterns and imagine alternatives. (30–40 min)
123 Metaphors 2	p. 61–64	Nancy loves this imagination-stretching process for uncovering new approaches to a stressful situation. (20–30 min)
124 911 Emergency Plan	p. 65–67	Whenever you make a presentation about stress there will always be people in the audience who are in crisis situations and need simple, practical, immediate techniques for making it through the day without panicking, bursting into tears, smoking, yelling at the kids, drinking or killing themselves. This exercise offers an anchor for desperate times. (20–30 min)
126 Go for the Gold	p. 73–81	Goal-setting is a universally applicable stress management tool. This skill-building exercise teaches a step-by-step process for organizing decisions toward specific, targeted goals. Ideal for all audiences. (30–40 min)
131 So What?	p. 102–104	Simple. Elegant. Effective. Memorable. (10–15 min)

©1994 Whole Person Press 210 W Michigan Duluth MN 55802   (800) 247-6789

144 Snap, Crackle, and Pop   This invigorating body-clapping routine
p. 132-133   gets the blood moving. Promotes interaction while it energizes the group.
(5–10 min)

ESPECIALLY FOR THE WORKPLACE

Most of the exercises in this volume are "generic" stress assessments, or management processes that can easily be adapted to a wide variety of settings. Occasionally you may be asked to specifically address the issue of workplace stress. If so, the exercises outlined below will be particularly applicable.

Workplace Exercises	Page	Comments (Timing)
117 On The Job Stress Grid	p. 25–32	Identify job stress and coping options. Chalktalk and worksheet grid covering three sources of job stress: relationships, environment, expectations. (25–40 min)
121 A Good Stress Manager	p. 47–54	Focus on coping attitudes/behaviors using the management metaphor and a group-generated assessment tool. (30–60 min)
122 Obligation Overload	p. 55–60	Standing up to pressure; saying YES and NO! Use **Merry-Go-Round** (Exercise 139, p. 122) as a lively warm-up/ demonstration. (45 min)
126 Go For The Gold	p. 73–81	Personal goal-setting techniques. (30–40 min)
133 Pat On The Back	p. 107–111	Affirmation experience for work groups. (20–30 min)
137 How To Swim With Sharks	p. 118–119	Managers love this reading. (5 min)

WINNING COMBINATIONS

Job Stress Presentation (60 min)

Begin your workshop with a topical icebreaker. Exercise111, **Quips and Quotes**, p. 5, can be shortened to 10 minutes by using only Steps 1 and 2 as an icebreaker. Participants choose catchy slogans that typify their approach to stress management. Or shorten Exercise 118, **Stress Attitudes Survey**, p. 33, to 10 minutes by choosing 2–3 statements for a quick warm-up vote (Steps 1–3). Then pick one statement particularly appropriate to your audience and setting for brief small group discussions (Step 4).

Use Exercise 117, **On The Job Stress Grid**, p. 25 (25–40 min), as the centerpiece of your presentation. Participants brainstorm sources of job stress, then use two worksheets to pinpoint their personal job "hot spots." The **Job Stress Grid** is a great tool for exploring workplace stressors. Expand the closing chalktalk on coping strategies to make a smooth transition to planning. Drop the homework.

Sometime during the session participants will mention difficult co-workers or a hostile work environment as sources of stress. When this issue comes up, stop and share the reading in Exercise 137, **How to Swim With Sharks**, p. 118 (5 min). It's a real gem.

Close your presentation with an effective planning process. Exercise 131, **So What?**, p. 102 (10–15 min), is simple, satisfying, and memorable. Or incorporate Exercise 130, **ABCDEFG Planner**, p. 97 (20–30 min), as a natural extension of the **Job Stress Grid**. Use the "hot spot" generated in Step 7 of the **Grid** as the "problem" in **Section A** of the **Planner**. Use the three "options for coping with organizational stress" from Step 8 as strategies for **Section E** of the **Planner**.

If you have time, add one or more energizers. Exercise 135, **Giraffe**, p. 113 (5 min), provides a quick stretch. Exercise 143, **Sigh of Relief**, p. 130 (3–5 min), is an easy but powerful stress reliever. Exercise 144, **Snap, Crackle, Pop**, p. 132 (5 min), is a lively three-person back massage that peps up a group.

Focus on the Physical: Stress and Relaxation (90 min)

Exercise 113, **Dear Me**, p. 12 (10–15 min), makes a nice reflective opening. Follow-up with the life-size stress assessment in Exercise 116, **Body Mapping**, p. 21 (30–45 min). Participants scan their bodies for tension, then pair up to map physical stress. Supplement the chalktalk with more information on the physical stress reaction and our inclination to ignore or override it.

Introduce the basic principles of relaxation as an antidote to stress using Exercise 129, **Biofeedback**, p. 92 (20–25 min). Miniature thermometers (Bio-dots) help people monitor fluctuating stress levels as they practice a simple relaxation routine. Again, beef up the opening chalktalk on the relaxation response.

Choose several additional relaxation routines to demonstrate the variety of tension-relievers available. This volume includes several: **135 Giraffe**, p. 113 (5 min), **136 Hot Tub**, p. 115 (8 min), **138 Human Knots**, p. 120 (5–10 min), **140 Microwave**, p. 124 (2 min), **142 Revitalize Your Eyes**, p. 128 (2–5 min each), **143 Sigh of Relief**, p. 130 (3–5 min), **144 Snap, Crackle, Pop**, p. 132 (5–10 min). If you have other volumes in the **Structured Exercises** series, you'll find even more options to choose from.

To close the session, use the companion process to your opening. Exercise 134, **Dear Me P.S.**, p. 112 (10–15 min), gives participants an opportunity to evaluate what they have learned and apply it to personal life situations.

Good Grief Workshop (1¹/₂–2¹/₂ hours)

Grief is a universal human experience — and a major source of stress and illness. Whether the loss is the death of a parent or a corporate restructuring, we are all vulnerable to the stressful lifetrap of saying "goodbye." Although this subject may seem too "personal" for intact groups in the work setting, we think the prevalence of relationships as "high stress" issues and the demonstrated correlation between grief and physical illness may make it worth the risk to explore this topic as an entry point to stress management.

Exercise 131, **Lifetrap 4: Good Grief**, p. 41 (60–90 min), provides an excellent structure for addressing the stress of letting go. This exercise assumes that the group has a general background knowledge about stress. If not, be sure to add some generic stress information to the opening chalktalk. To extend the process or to include a more in-depth coping skill presentation and practice, try these "natural companions."

Use Exercise 109B, **Barometer**, p. 2 (5–10 min, 1 min per person—divide into groups of 4–8), as an icebreaker. This quick introduction helps people focus on their recent life experience.

Be sure to read the **Mustard Seed Parable**, Exercise 141 (p. 126, 5 min), after you're opening chalktalk. It's an absolute classic.

Follow up your "closing" chalktalk with an exploration of self-disclosure as an appropriate skill for coping with grief using Exercise 128, **Open Up**, p. 87 (45–50 min). The list of "helping" resources generated by the group may be especially valuable.

A closing planning/implementation process will promote better transfer of learning. Try Exercise 124, **911 Emergency Plan**, p. 65 (20-30 min), an outstanding exercise for developing a personalized plan for managing crisis situations so common to grief reactions. Or substitute Exercise 131, **So What?**, p. 102 (10–15 min), or Exercise 134, **Dear Me P.S.**, p. 112 (10–15 min), as described above.

ANNOTATED INDEXES

©1994 Whole Person Press 210 W Michigan Duluth MN 55802   (800) 247-6789

Index to DEMONSTRATIONS

©1994 Whole Person Press 210 W Michigan Duluth MN 55802   (800) 247-6789

Index to PHYSICAL ENERGIZERS

©1994 Whole Person Press 210 W Michigan Duluth MN 55802   (800) 247-6789

Index to MENTAL ENERGIZERS

©1994 Whole Person Press 210 W Michigan Duluth MN 55802   (800) 247-6789

Index to RELAXATION ROUTINES

©1994 Whole Person Press 210 W Michigan Duluth MN 55802   (800) 247-6789

CONTRIBUTORS

Glenn Q Bannerman, President of Bannerman Family Celebration Services, Inc., Box 399, Montreat NC 28757. 704/669-7323. Professor Emeritus of the Presbyterian School of Christian Education, Richmond VA. Glenn is a specialist in church recreation and outdoor education. He has conducted workshops throughout the US, as well as overseas in 12 foreign countries. His group experiences range from movement exercises and clog dancing to gaming, puppetry, crafts, and camping. He is co-author of **Guide for Recreation Leaders**, and author of five LP American Mountain Music and Dance records.

Kent D Beeler, EdD. 6025 Compton Street, Indianapolis IN 46220-2003. 317/259-8064. Kent is an active advocate of wellness at the college and university level. His experiential workshops have been popular with campus and professional groups interested in personal lifestyle promotion. Kent is a year-round, recreational runner, and has served on the Directorate Body, American College Personnel Assoc Comm VIII: Wellness.

Richard Boyum, EdD. Senior Psychologist, University of Wisconsin–Eau Claire, Eau Claire WI 54702. 715/836-5521 (w), 715/874-6222 (h). Dr Boyum has been a practicing psychologist, counselor, and teacher at the University of Wisconsin-Eau Claire since 1973. His specialities include the use of guided imagery and metaphor in creating healthier behaviors. He also works with individuals, families and organizations in creating behavioral changes through the use of both individual and systems models.

Lucia Capacchione, MA, PhD. PO Box 1355, Cambria CA 93428. 310/281-7495 (w), 805/546-1424 (h). Lucia is an art therapist, seminar leader, and corporate consultant. She is the author of nine books, including The **Creative Journal** (with versions for adults, teens and children), **The Well-Being Journal, Lighten Up Your Body, Lighten Up Your Life**, and **The Picture of Health**. After healing herself from a collagen disease through creative journaling, Lucia has dedicated her professional life to researching right brain approaches to healing and empowering individuals and organizations with new vision and innovative healing alternatives. Her best-known books, **The Power of Your Other Hand** and **Recovery of Your Inner Child**, open new doors to self-health.

Emmajane S Finney, MDiv. 224 W. Packer Ave, Bethlehem PA, 18015. 215/865-9777. Em is a Parish Minister in the United Church of Christ. She has special interests in Christian Education, women's spirituality, leadership of worship, and church-based community organization.

Joel Goodman, EdD. Director, The HUMOR Project, 110 Spring Street, Saratoga Springs NY 12866. 518/587-8770. Joel is a popular speaker, consultant and seminar leader who has presented to over 500,000 corporate managers, health care leaders, educators, and other helping professionals throughout the U.S. and abroad. Author of 8 books, Joel publishes **Laughing Matters** magazine and

HUMOResources mail order bookstore catalog, and sponsors the annual international conference on "The Positive Power of Humor and Creativity."

Krysta Eryn Kavenaugh, MA, CSP. 955 Lake Drive, St Paul MN 55120. 800/ 829-8437 (w) 612/725-6763 (h). Krysta is a speaker, trainer, and consultant. Her mission is to take people "into the heart of wisdom." She speaks with style, substance, and spirit. She is also the managing editor of **Marriage** magazine. Her favorite keynote topic is "Romancing Yourself: Taking Care of You is Taking Care of Business." She also speaks on proactive support teams, turning adversity to our advantage, ecology, and customized business topics.

Pat Miller, 1211 N Basswood Ave, Duluth MN 55811. 218/722-9361. Pat runs her own consulting and teaching business, Pat Miller Training and Development. She teaches workshops, conducts on-sight team building sessions, facilitates retreats, and mediates conflict in the workplace. Her areas of expertise include communication skills, conflict resolution, team development, self-esteem, and stress management.

Lyn Clark Pegg, Lutheran Social Services of Minnesota-Duluth, 424 W Superior St, Duluth MN 55802. 218/726-4769. Lyn has lived the career development process. Twenty years, and seven career decisions later, she found out the color of her parachute at Lutheran Social Service. As Director of the Duluth office, she enjoys the best of all worlds—administration, counseling, professional consultation and community education. All in the context of a Minnesotan culture that affirms human services. Wonderful!

Sandy Queen, Director, LIFEWORKS, PO Box 2668, Columbia MD 21045. 401/ 796-5310. Sandy is the founder and director of Lifeworks, Inc., a training/ counseling firm that specializes in helping people take a better look at their lives through humor, laughter, and play. Author of **Wellness Activities for Youth** She has developed many innovative programs in the areas of stress-reduction, humor, children's wellness, and self-esteem.

Gloria Singer, ACSW. 43 Rivermoor Landing, 125 Main Street, New Market NH 03857-1640. 603/659-7530. Gloria's background as a social worker and educator are valuable assets in her position as Director of E.A.P. Services, resource management consultants in Salem NH. In that capacity she has enjoyed designing site-specific programs in stress management and wellness as well as training, counseling and group work with employees and their families.

Mary O'Brien Sippel, RN MS. Licensed Psychologist, 22 East St Andrews, Duluth MN 55803. 218/723-6130 (w) 218/724-5935 (h). Educated as a nurse, Mary has spent over 25 years working the field of community health and education. She has conducted seminars on stress management, burnout prevention, and wellness promotion throughout the U.S. She is currently a personal counselor and adjunct faculty member at the College of St Scholastica, Duluth MN. She is also working on **Wildflower Adventures**, a book on getting food and weight in a healthy perspective for children.

Ruth Strom-McCutcheon, RN, MS, CNP. Student Health Service, University of Minnesota-Duluth, Duluth MN 55812. 218/726-8155 (w), 218/727-5842 (h). Ruth is a nurse practitioner specializing in women's health care. Her work for over 15 years in the area of eating disorders, counseling groups and individuals, led her back to graduate school in psych-mental health nursing. Her work at the university provides her with a great deal of variety and a chance to be creative as you may find her at the clinic, the dorms, a classroom, or in an athletic locker room! Presentations: stress management, body image, assertiveness, self-esteem, eating disorders, nutrition.

Larry Tobin, MA. Jade Mist Press, 2529 SE 64th, Portland OR 97026. Larry is a special educator, school psychologist, and national trainer on working with troubled children. He has authored **What Do You Do with a Child Like This?**, **62 Ways to Create Change in the Lives of Troubled Children**, and **Time Well Spent**, a year-long stress management planner.

FUTURE CONTRIBUTORS

If you have developed an exciting, effective structured exercise you'd like to share with other trainers in the field of stress or wellness, please send it to us for consideration, using the following guidelines:

- Your entry should be written in a format similar to those in this volume.

- Contributors must either guarantee that the materials they submit are not previously copyrighted or provide a copyright release for inclusion in the Whole Person **Structured Exercises** series.

- When you have adapted the work of others, please acknowledge the original source of ideas or activities.

©1994 Whole Person Press 210 W Michigan Duluth MN 55802   (800) 247-6789

EDITORS

All exercises in this volume not specifically attributed to other contributors are the creative efforts of the editors, who have been designing, collecting, and experimenting with structured processes in their teaching, training and consultation work since the late 1960s.

Nancy Loving Tubesing, EdD, holds a masters degree in group counseling and a doctorate in counselor education. She served as editor of the *Society for Wholistic Medicine's* monograph series and articulated the principles of whole person health care in the monograph, **Philosophical Assumptions**. Faculty Associate and Product Development Coordinator at Whole Person Associates, Nancy is always busy compiling and testing teaching designs for future **Structured Exercises** volumes.

Donald A Tubesing, MDiv, PhD, designer of the classic **Stress Skills** seminar and author of the best-selling **Kicking Your Stress Habits**, has been a pioneer in the movement to reintegrate body, mind, and spirit in health care delivery. With his entrepreneurial spirit and background in theology, psychology, and education, Don brings the whole person perspective to his writing, speaking, and consultation in business and industry, government agencies, health care and human service systems.

Nancy and Don have collaborated on many writing projects over the years, beginning with a small-group college orientation project in 1970 and including two self-help books on whole person wellness, **The Caring Question** (Minneapolis: Augsburg, 1983) and **Seeking Your Healthy Balance** (Duluth: Whole Person Press, 1991) and a score of unusual relaxation audiotapes.

The Tubesings have specialized in developing creative stress management programs and packages for client groups such as the national YMCA (8-session course, **The Y's Way to Stress Management**) and Aid Association for Lutherans (**The Stress Kit** multimedia resource for families).

Their most recent efforts have been directed toward combining the process-oriented approach of the **Structured Exercises** series with the power of video. The resulting three six-session interactive video courses, **WellAware**, **Manage It!**, and **Managing Job Stress**, include participant booklets with worksheets that stimulate personal reflection and application of principles to specific situations, as well as a step-by-step leader manual for guiding group interaction.

WORKSHOPS-IN-A-BOOK

KICKING YOUR STRESS HABITS:
A Do-it-yourself Guide to Coping with Stress
Donald A. Tubesing, PhD

Over a quarter of a million people have found ways to deal with their everyday stress by using **Kicking Your Stress Habits**. This workshop-in-a-book actively involves the reader in assessing stressful patterns and developing more effective coping strategies with helpful "Stop and Reflect" sections in each chapter.

The 10-step planning process and 20 skills for managing stress make **Kicking Your Stress Habits** an ideal text for stress management classes in many different settings, from hospitals to universities and for a wide variety of groups.

❏ K / Kicking Your Stress Habits / 14.95

SEEKING YOUR HEALTHY BALANCE:
A Do-it-yourself Guide to Whole Person Well-being
Donald A. Tubesing, PhD and Nancy Loving Tubesing, EdD

Where can you find the time and energy to "do it all" without sacrificing your health and well-being? **Seeking Your Healthy Balance** helps the reader discover how to make changes toward a more balanced lifestyle by learning effective ways to juggle work, self, and others; clarifying self-care options; and discovering and setting their own personal priorities.

Seeking Your Healthy Balance asks the questions and helps readers find their own answers.

❏ HB / Seeking Your Healthy Balance / 14.95

©1994 Whole Person Press 210 W Michigan Duluth MN 55802   (800) 247-6789

STRUCTURED EXERCISES
IN STRESS MANAGEMENT—VOLUMES 1-4
Nancy Loving Tubesing, EdD and Donald A. Tubesing, PhD, Editors

Each book in this four-volume series contains 36 ready-to-use teaching modules that involve the participant—as a whole person—in learning how to manage stress more effectively.

Each exercise is carefully designed by top stress-management professionals. Instructions are clearly written and field-tested so that even beginning trainers can smoothly lead a group through warm-up and closure, reflection and planning, and action and interaction—all with minimum preparation time.

Each Stress Handbook is brimming with practical ideas that you can weave into your own teaching designs or mix and match to develop new programs for varied settings, audiences, and time frames. In each volume you'll find **Icebreakers, Stress Assessments, Management Strategies, Skill Builders, Action Planners, Closing Processes** and **Group Energizers**—all with a special focus on stress management.

STRUCTURED EXERCISES
IN WELLNESS PROMOTION—VOLUMES 1-4
Nancy Loving Tubesing, EdD and Donald A. Tubesing, PhD, Editors

Discover the Wellness Handbooks—from the wellness pioneers at Whole Person Associates. Each volume in this innovative series includes 36 experiential learning activities that focus on whole person health—body, mind, spirit, emotions, relationships, and lifestyle.

The exercises, developed by an interdisciplinary pool of leaders in the wellness movement nationwide, actively encourage people to adopt wellness-oriented attitudes and to develop more responsible self-care patterns.

All process designs in the Wellness Handbooks are clearly explained and have been thoroughly field-tested with diverse audiences so that trainers can use them with confidence. **Icebreakers, Wellness Explorations, Self-Care Strategies, Action Planners, Closings** and **Group Energizers** are all ready-to-go—including reproducible worksheets, scripts, and chalktalk outlines—for the busy professional who wants to develop unique wellness programs without spending oodles of time in preparation.

©1994 Whole Person Press 210 W Michigan Duluth MN 55802   (800) 247-6789

STRUCTURED EXERCISES IN STRESS AND WELLNESS ARE AVAILABLE IN TWO FORMATS

LOOSE-LEAF FORMAT (8 1/2" x 11")

The loose-leaf, 3-ring binder format provides you with maximum flexiblity. The binder gives you plenty of room to add your own adaptations, workshop outlines, or notes right where you need them. The index tabs offer quick and easy access to each section of exercises, and the generous margins allow plenty of room for notes. In addition an extra set of the full-size worksheets and handouts are packaged separately for convenient duplication.

SOFTCOVER FORMAT (6" x 9")

The softcover format is a perfect companion to the loose-leaf version. This smaller book fits easily into your briefcase or bag, and the binding has been designed to remain open on your desk or lecturn. Worksheets and handouts can be enlarged and photocopied for distribution to your participants, or you can purchase sets of worksheet masters.

WORKSHEET MASTERS

The Worksheet Masters for the two Structured Exercise series offer full-size (8 1/2" x 11") photocopy masters. All of the worksheets and handouts for each volume are reproduced in easy-to-read print with professional graphics. All you need to do to complete your workshop preparation is run them through a copier.

Structured Exercises in Stress Management

- ❏ **Loose-Leaf Edition—Volume 1-4 / $54.95 each**
- ❏ **Softcover Edition—Volume 1-4 / $29.95 each**
- ❏ **Worksheet Masters—Volume 1-4 / $9.95 each**

Structured Exercises in Wellness Promotion

- ❏ **Loose-Leaf Edition—Volume 1-4 / $54.95 each**
- ❏ **Softcover Edition—Volume 1-4 / $29.95 each**
- ❏ **Worksheet Masters—Volume 1-4 / $9.95 each**

ADDITIONAL GROUP PROCESS RESOURCES

Our group process exercises are designed to address the whole person—physical, emotional, mental, spiritual, and social. Developed for trainers by trainers, all of these group process resources are ready-to-use. The novice trainer will find everything they need to get started, and the expert trainer will discover new ideas and concepts to add to their existing programs.

All of the exercises encourage interaction between the leader and the participants, as well as among the participants. Each exercise includes everything you need to present a meaningful program: goals, optimal group size, time frame, materials list, and the complete process instructions.

PLAYFUL ACTIVITIES FOR POWERFUL PRESENTATIONS
Bruce Williamson

This book contains 40 fun exercises designed to fit any group or topic. These exercises will help you:

- build teamwork
- encourage laughter and playfulness
- relieve stress and tension
- free up the imaginations of participants

  ❏ **PAP / Playful Activities for Powerful Presentations / $19.95**

WORKING WITH GROUPS FROM DYSFUNCTIONAL FAMILIES
Cheryl Hetherington

This collection of 29 proven group activities is designed to heal the pain that results from growing up in or living in a dysfunctional family. With these exercises you can:

- promote healing
- build self-esteem
- encourage sharing
- help participants acknowledge their feelings

WORKING WITH GROUPS FROM DYSFUNCTIONAL FAMILIES REPRODUCIBLE WORKSHEET MASTERS

A complete package of full-size (8 1/2" x 11") photocopy masters that include all the worksheets and handouts from **Working with Groups from Dysfunctional Families** is available to you. Use the masters for easy duplication of the handouts for each participant.

  ❏ **DFH / Working with Groups from Dysfunctional Families / $19.95**
  ❏ **DFW / Dysfunctional Families Worksheet Masters / $9.95**

WORKING WITH WOMEN'S GROUPS Volumes 1 & 2
Louise Yolton Eberhardt

The two volumes of **Working with Women's Groups** have been completely revised and updated. These exercises will help women explore issues that are of perennial concern as well as today's hot topics.

- consciousness-raising (volume 1)
- self-discovery (volume 1)
- assertiveness training (volume 1)
- sexuality issues (volume 2)
- women of color (volume 2)
- leadership skills training (volume 2)

> ❏ **WG1 / Working with Women's Groups—Volume 1 / $19.95**
> ❏ **WG2 / Working with Women's Groups—Volume 2 / $19.95**

WORKING WITH MEN'S GROUPS
Roger Karsk and Bill Thomas

Also revised and updated, this volume is a valuable resource for anyone working with men's groups. The exercises cover a variety of topics, including:

- self discovery
- parenting
- conflict
- intimacy

> ❏ **MG / Working with Men's Groups / $19.95**

WELLNESS ACTIVITIES FOR YOUTH Volumes 1 & 2
Sandy Queen

Each volume of **Wellness Activities for Youth** helps leaders teach children and teenagers about wellness with an emphasis on FUN. The concepts include:

- values
- stress and coping
- self-esteem
- personal well-being

WELLNESS ACTIVITIES FOR YOUTH WORKSHEET MASTERS

Complete packages of full-size (8 1/2" x 11") photocopy masters that include all the worksheets and handouts from **Wellness Activities for Youth Volumes 1 and 2** are available to you. Use the masters for easy duplication of the handouts for each participant.

> ❏ **WY1 / Wellness Activities for Youth Volume 1 / $19.95**
> ❏ **WY2 / Wellness Activities for Youth Volume 2 / $19.95**
> ❏ **WY1W / Wellness Activities for Youth V.1 Worksheet Masters / $9.95**
> ❏ **WY2W / Wellness Activities for Youth V. 2 Worksheet Masters / $9.95**

©1994 Whole Person Press 210 W Michigan Duluth MN 55802   (800) 247-6789

RELAXATION AUDIOTAPES

Perhaps you're an old hand at relaxation, looking for new ideas. Or maybe you're a beginner, just testing the waters. Whatever your relaxation needs, Whole Person tapes provide a whole family of techniques for reducing physical and mental stress. To assist in your decision-making, you may want to know more about different types of relaxation.

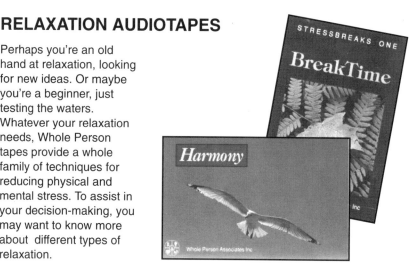

We offer six different types of relaxation techniques in our twenty-one tapes. The Whole Person series ranges from simple breathing and stretching exercises, to classic autogenic and progressive relaxation sequences, to guided meditations and whimsical daydreams. All are carefully crafted to promote whole person relaxation—body, mind, and spirit. We also provide a line of music-only tapes, composed specifically for relaxation.

SENSATIONAL RELAXATION

When stress piles up, it becomes a heavy load both physically and emotionally. These full-length relaxation experiences will teach you techniques that can be used whenever you feel that stress is getting out of control. Choose one you like and repeat it daily until it becomes second nature then recall that technique whenever you need it.

- ❏ **CD / Countdown to Relaxation / $9.95**
- ❏ **DS / Daybreak / Sundown / $9.95**
- ❏ **TDB / Take a Deep Breath / $9.95**
- ❏ **RLX / Relax . . . Let Go . . . Relax / $9.95**
- ❏ **SRL / StressRelease / $9.95**
- ❏ **WRM / Warm and Heavy / $9.95**

STRESS BREAKS

Do you need a short energy booster or a quick stress reliever? If you don't know what type of relaxation you like, or if you are new to guided relaxation techniques, try one of our Stress Breaks for a quick refocusing or change of pace any time of the day.

- ❏ **BT / BreakTime / $9.95**
- ❏ **NT / Natural Tranquilizers / $9.95**

DAYDREAMS

Escape from the stress around you with guided tours to beautiful places. Picture yourself traveling to the ocean, sitting in a park, luxuriating in the view from the majestic mountains, or enjoying the solitude and serenity of a cozy cabin. The 10-minute escapes included in our Daydream tapes will lead your imagination away from your everyday cares so you can resume your tasks relaxed and comforted.

- ❑ **DD1 / Daydreams 1: Getaways / $9.95**
- ❑ **DD2 / Daydreams 2: Peaceful Places / $9.95**

GUIDED MEDITATION

Take a step beyond relaxation and discover the connection between body and mind with guided meditation. The imagery in our full-length meditations will help you discover your strengths, find healing, make positive life changes, and recognize your inner wisdom.

- ❑ **IH / Inner Healing / $9.95**
- ❑ **PE / Personal Empowering / $9.95**
- ❑ **HBT / Healthy Balancing / $9.95**
- ❑ **SPC / Spiritual Centering / $9.95**

WILDERNESS DAYDREAMS

Discover the healing power of nature with the four tapes in the Wilderness Daydreams series. The eight special journeys will transport you from your harried, stressful surroundings to the peaceful serenity of words and water.

- ❑ **WD1 / Canoe / Rain / $9.95**
- ❑ **WD2 / Island /Spring / $9.95**
- ❑ **WD3 / Campfire / Stream / $9.95**
- ❑ **WD4 / Sailboat / Pond / $9.95**

MUSIC ONLY

No relaxation program would be complete without relaxing melodies that can be played as background to a prepared script or that can be enjoyed as you practice a technique you have already learned. Steven Eckels composed his melodies specifically for relaxation. These "musical prayers for healing" will calm your body, mind, and spirit.

- ❑ **T / Tranquility / $9.95**
- ❑ **H / Harmony / $9.95**
- ❑ **S / Serenity / $9.95**

Titles can be combined for discounts!

QUANTITY DISCOUNT			
1 - 9	10 - 49	50 - 99	100+
$9.95	$8.95	$7.96	CALL

©1994 Whole Person Press 210 W Michigan Duluth MN 55802   (800) 247-6789

RELAXATION RESOURCES

Many trainers and workshop leaders have discovered the benefits of relaxation and visualization in healing the body, mind, and spirit.

30 SCRIPTS FOR RELAXATION, IMAGERY, AND INNER HEALING
Julie Lusk

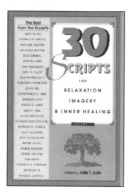

These two volumes are collections of relaxation scripts created by trainers for trainers. The 30 scripts in each of the two volumes have been professionally-tested and fine-tuned so they are ready to use for both novice and expert trainers.

Help your participants change their behavior, enhance their self-esteem, discover inner, private places, and heal themselves through simple trainer-led guided imagery scripts. Both volumes include information on how to use the scripts, suggestions for tailoring them to your specific needs and audience, and information on how to successfully incorporate guided imagery into your existing programs.

❑ **30S / 30 Scripts for Relaxation, Imagery, and Inner Healing—Volume 1 / $19.95**
❑ **30S2 / 30 Scripts for Relaxation, Imagery, and Inner Healing—Volume 2 / $19.95**

INQUIRE WITHIN
Andrew Schwartz

Use visualization to make positive changes in your life. The 24 visualization experiences in **Inquire Within** will help participants enhance their creativity, heal inner pain, learn to relax, and deal with conflict. Each visualization includes questions at the end of the process that encourage deeper reflection and a better understanding of the exercise and the response it invokes.

❑ **IW / Inquire Within / $19.95**

ORDER FORM

Name _____

Address _____

City _____

State/Zip _____

Area Code/Telephone _____

Please make checks payable to:
Whole Person Associates Inc
210 West Michigan
Duluth MN 55802-1908
FAX: 1-218-727-0505
TOLL FREE: 1-800-247-6789

Books / Workshops-In-A-Book

____ Kicking Your Stress Habits .... $14.95 _____

____ Seeking Your Healthy Balance .... $14.95 _____

Structured Exercises in Stress Management Series—Volumes 1-4

____ Stress Softcover Edition .... Vol 1 ___ Vol 2 ___ Vol 3 ___ Vol 4 ___ $29.95 _____

____ Stress Loose-Leaf Edition .... Vol 1 ___ Vol 2 ___ Vol 3 ___ Vol 4 ___ $54.95 _____

____ Stress Worksheets Masters .... Vol 1 ___ Vol 2 ___ Vol 3 ___ Vol 4 ___ $9.95 _____

Structured Exercises in Wellness Promotion Series—Volumes 1-4

____ Wellness Softcover Edition .... Vol 1 ___ Vol 2 ___ Vol 3 ___ Vol 4 ___ $29.95 _____

____ Wellness Loose-Leaf Edition .... Vol 1 ___ Vol 2 ___ Vol 3 ___ Vol 4 ___ $54.95 _____

____ Wellness Worksheets Masters .... Vol 1 ___ Vol 2 ___ Vol 3 ___ Vol 4 ___ $9.95 _____

Group Process Resources

____ Playful Activities for Powerful Presentations .... $19.95 _____

____ Working with Groups from Dysfunctional Families .... $19.95 _____

____ Working with Groups from Dysfunctional Families Worksheet Masters .... $ 9.95 _____

____ Working with Women's Groups .... Vol 1 ___ Vol 2 ___ $19.95 _____

____ Working with Men's Groups .... $19.95 _____

____ Wellness Activities for Youth .... Vol 1 ___ Vol 2 ___ $19.95 _____

____ Wellness Activities for Youth Worksheet Master .... Vol 1 ___ Vol 2 ___ $9.95 _____

Relaxation Audiotapes

____ BreakTime .... $ 9.95 _____

____ Countdown to Relaxation .... $ 9.95 _____

____ Daybreak/Sundown .... $ 9.95 _____

____ Daydreams 1: Getaways .... $ 9.95 _____

____ Daydreams 2: Peaceful Places .... $ 9.95 _____

____ Harmony (music only) .... $ 9.95 _____

____ Healthy Balancing .... $ 9.95 _____

____ Inner Healing .... $ 9.95 _____

____ Natural Tranquilizers .... $ 9.95 _____

____ Personal Empowering .... $ 9.95 _____

____ Relax . . . Let Go . . . Relax .... $ 9.95 _____

____ Serenity (music only) .... $ 9.95 _____

____ Spiritual Centering .... $ 9.95 _____

____ StressRelease .... $ 9.95 _____

____ Take a Deep Breath .... $ 9.95 _____

____ Tranquility (music only) .... $ 9.95 _____

____ Warm and Heavy .... $ 9.95 _____

____ Wilderness DD 1: Canoe/Rain .... $ 9.95 _____

____ Wilderness DD 2: Island/Spring .... $ 9.95 _____

____ Wilderness DD 3: Campfire/Stream .... $ 9.95 _____

____ Wilderness DD 4: Sailboat/Pond .... $ 9.95 _____

Relaxation Resources

____ 30 Scripts—Volume 1 .... $19.95 _____

____ 30 Scripts—Volume 2 .... $19.95 _____

____ Inquire Within .... $19.95 _____

My check is enclosed. **(US funds only)**

Please charge my _____ Visa _____ Mastercard

_____

Exp date _____

Signature _____

SUBTOTAL _____

TAX (MN residents 6.5%) _____

7% GST-Canadian customers only _____

***SHIPPING** _____

GRAND TOTAL _____

800-247-6789

** **SHIPPING**. $5.00 ($8.00 outside U.S.)
Please call us for quotes on UPS 3rd Day,
2nd Day or Next Day Air.

ORDER FORM

Name _____

Address _____

City _____

State/Zip _____

Area Code/Telephone _____

Please make checks payable to:
Whole Person Associates Inc
210 West Michigan
Duluth MN 55802-1908
FAX: 1-218-727-0505
TOLL FREE: 1-800-247-6789

Books / Workshops-In-A-Book

___ Kicking Your Stress Habits .... $14.95 _____

___ Seeking Your Healthy Balance .... $14.95 _____

Structured Exercises in Stress Management Series—Volumes 1-4

___ Stress Softcover Edition .... Vol 1 ___ Vol 2 ___ Vol 3 ___ Vol 4 ___ $29.95 _____

___ Stress Loose-Leaf Edition .... Vol 1 ___ Vol 2 ___ Vol 3 ___ Vol 4 ___ $54.95 _____

___ Stress Worksheets Masters .... Vol 1 ___ Vol 2 ___ Vol 3 ___ Vol 4 ___ $9.95 _____

Structured Exercises in Wellness Promotion Series—Volumes 1-4

___ Wellness Softcover Edition .... Vol 1 ___ Vol 2 ___ Vol 3 ___ Vol 4 ___ $29.95 _____

___ Wellness Loose-Leaf Edition .... Vol 1 ___ Vol 2 ___ Vol 3 ___ Vol 4 ___ $54.95 _____

___ Wellness Worksheets Masters .... Vol 1 ___ Vol 2 ___ Vol 3 ___ Vol 4 ___ $9.95 _____

Group Process Resources

___ Playful Activities for Powerful Presentations .... $19.95 _____

___ Working with Groups from Dysfunctional Families .... $19.95 _____

___ Working with Groups from Dysfunctional Families Worksheet Masters .... $ 9.95 _____

___ Working with Women's Groups .... Vol 1 ___ Vol 2 ___ $19.95 _____

___ Working with Men's Groups .... $19.95 _____

___ Wellness Activities for Youth .... Vol 1 ___ Vol 2 ___ $19.95 _____

___ Wellness Activities for Youth Worksheet Master .... Vol 1 ___ Vol 2 ___ $9.95 _____

Relaxation Audiotapes

___ BreakTime .... $ 9.95 _____

___ Countdown to Relaxation .... $ 9.95 _____

___ Daybreak/Sundown .... $ 9.95 _____

___ Daydreams 1: Getaways .... $ 9.95 _____

___ Daydreams 2: Peaceful Places .... $ 9.95 _____

___ Harmony (music only) .... $ 9.95 _____

___ Healthy Balancing .... $ 9.95 _____

___ Inner Healing .... $ 9.95 _____

___ Natural Tranquilizers .... $ 9.95 _____

___ Personal Empowering .... $ 9.95 _____

___ Relax . . . Let Go . . . Relax .... $ 9.95 _____

___ Serenity (music only) .... $ 9.95 _____

___ Spiritual Centering .... $ 9.95 _____

___ StressRelease .... $ 9.95 _____

___ Take a Deep Breath .... $ 9.95 _____

___ Tranquility (music only) .... $ 9.95 _____

___ Warm and Heavy .... $ 9.95 _____

___ Wilderness DD 1: Canoe/Rain .... $ 9.95 _____

___ Wilderness DD 2: Island/Spring .... $ 9.95 _____

___ Wilderness DD 3: Campfire/Stream .... $ 9.95 _____

___ Wilderness DD 4: Sailboat/Pond .... $ 9.95 _____

Relaxation Resources

___ 30 Scripts—Volume 1 .... $19.95 _____

___ 30 Scripts—Volume 2 .... $19.95 _____

___ Inquire Within .... $19.95 _____

My check is enclosed. **(US funds only)**

Please charge my_____Visa _____Mastercard

_____

Exp date _____

Signature _____

SUBTOTAL _____

TAX (MN residents 6.5%) _____

7% GST-Canadian customers only _____

**SHIPPING* _____

GRAND TOTAL _____

800-247-6789

** **SHIPPING**. $5.00 ($8.00 outside U.S.)
Please call us for quotes on UPS 3rd Day,
2nd Day or Next Day Air.

About Whole Person Associates

At Whole Person Associates, we're 100% committed to providing stress and wellness materials that involve participants and have a "whole person" focus—body, mind, spirit, and relationships.

That's our mission and it's very important to us— but it doesn't tell the whole story. Behind the products in our catalog is a company full of people—and *that's* what really makes us who we are.

ABOUT THE OWNERS

Whole Person Associates was created by the vision of two people: Donald A. Tubesing, PhD, and Nancy Loving Tubesing, EdD. Since way back in 1970, Don and Nancy have been active in the stress management / wellness movement—consulting, leading seminars, writing, and publishing. Most of our early products were the result of their creativity and expertise.

Living proof that you can "stay evergreen," Don and Nancy remain the driving force behind the company and are still very active in developing new products that touch people's lives.

ABOUT THE COMPANY

Whole Person Associates was "born" in Duluth, Minnesota, and we remain committed to our lovely city on the shore of Lake Superior. All of our operations are here, which makes communication between departments much easier!

We've grown since our beginnings, but at a steady pace—we're interested in sustainable growth that allows us to keep our down-to-earth orientation—and put the same high quality into every product we offer.

ABOUT OUR EMPLOYEES

Speaking of down-to-earth, that's a requirement for each and every one of our employees. We're all product consultants, which means that anyone who answers the phone can probably answer your questions (if they can't, they'll find someone who can.)

We focus on helping you find the products that fit your needs. And we've found that the best way to do that is to hire friendly and resourceful people.

ABOUT OUR ASSOCIATES

Who are the "associates" in Whole Person Associates? They're the trainers, authors, musicians, and others who have developed much of the material you see on these pages. We're always on the lookout for high-quality products that reflect our "whole person" philosophy and fill a need for our customers.

Most of our products were developed by experts who are the tops in their fields, and we're very proud to be associated with them.

ABOUT OUR CUSTOMERS

Finally, we wouldn't have a reason to exist without you, our customers. We've met some of you, and we've talked to many more of you on the phone. We are always aware that without you, there would be no Whole Person Associates.

That's why we'd love to hear from you! Let us know what you think of our products—how you use them in your work, what additional products you'd like to see, and what shortcomings you've noted. Write us or call on our toll-free line. We're waiting for your call!